Praise for *Hurt Healing Healed*

"This is THE guide to self-healing, breaking through to abundance and supercharging your manifestation! Emma Mumford's tools really work and will get you the manifestation results you want."

Mel Robbins, author of *New York Times* bestseller *The High 5 Habit*

"Emma Mumford presents an essential guide for those ready to embark upon the path to high vibes and healing."

Kyle Gray, bestselling author of *Raise Your Vibration*

"A fantastic book on how to effectively identify and release limiting beliefs! Emma's tools and practices throughout are unique, powerful and get you manifesting quickly – highly recommend!"

Amy Leigh Mercree , bestselling author of 16 books including *The Healing Home*

"Doing the inner work isn't easy, but knowing how to navigate it definitely helps! Through relatable and heartwarming stories, powerful insights and practical processes, *Hurt Healing Healed* shares a framework for embracing our feelings and clearing our obstacles, on the way to manifesting our desires."

George Lizos, bestselling author of *Protect Your Light* and *Lightworkers Gotta Work*

"The number one thing that blocks us from experiencing a joyful, abundant life is unprocessed pain. This amazing book will help you to identify and heal subconscious trauma. Armed with self-awareness you can attain the wellbeing that you desire. A fantastic read."

Claire Stone, international psychic and bestselling author of *The Female Archangels*

EMMA MUMFORD

Hurt Healing Healed

Release Limiting
Beliefs, Fears & Blocks
to Supercharge Your
Manifestation

WATKINS
Sharing Wisdom Since 1893

Hurt, Healing, Healed
Emma Mumford

First published in the UK and USA in 2022 by
Watkins, an imprint of Watkins Media Limited
Unit 11, Shepperton House,
83–93 Shepperton Road
London N1 3DF

enquiries@watkinspublishing.com

Publisher: Fiona Robertson
Commissioning Editor: Anya Hayes
Assistant Editor: Brittany Willis
Head of Design: Karen Smith
Design concept: Kieryn Tyler
Production: Uzma Taj

A CIP record for this book is available from the British Library

ISBN: 978-1-78678-679-1 (Paperback)
ISBN: 978-1-78678-678-4 (eBook)

10 9 8 7 6 5 4 3 2 1

Typeset by Lapiz

Printed in United Kingdom by TJ Books Ltd

www.watkinspublishing.com

For Luna, AB, my friends and my loved ones – thank you for reminding me what unconditional love is and for helping guide me home to myself and peace.

This is for all of you navigating this journey of inner healing and coming home to yourself. I really hope this book brings you the same peace and abundance as the journey did for me.

Other Books by the Author:

Positively Wealthy

The Positively Wealthy Journal

Spiritual Queen

Contents

Introduction

I started writing this book back in May 2020 when the first global lockdown happened and COVID-19 made its entrance in the world. It was a year that changed everything for every single human being, and looking back, I realize now just how much we have all grown and evolved since then. The words I wrote back then feel like a lifetime ago today, and this book has turned out to be part of an expansive journey, even though I didn't fully understand its direction until now.

I've wanted to write this book since I finished writing *Spiritual Queen*, but then my book *Positively Wealthy* needed to come through first and, thinking about it, I can see why this was important. I also knew this new book would be about love, but it's only now in this new world, this new reality we're all in, that I can see the book's theme is really about returning to a state of unconditional love through healing. It's about releasing our limiting beliefs and fears, and removing any blocks or resistance that stand in the way of manifesting abundance and experiencing unconditional love for ourselves and others. In this book, you will find a powerful three-step process to help you achieve this and welcome the healing it brings into your own life.

According to numerology, I'm a Life Path 33, which means that my ultimate lessons and purpose here in this lifetime are about learning unconditional love in all its forms. This has certainly been an experience, I can tell you! And something which I'm sure I will continue to learn in positive ways until my last breath – and which I am so happy to be sharing with you now.

When I was going through the depths of my own inner work journey, I craved books that would help me deal with limiting beliefs and fears, but sadly – apart from the psychology books and academic books on inner child work that I studied – I didn't have much luck. This is what ultimately led me to write *Hurt, Healing, Healed*. When so many of you kept asking me for book recommendations on shadow work and inner work, I decided that I'd write the book I'd needed during my own healing journey. There are no other books like this one and I hope it will be the perfect spiritual, practical and cognitive book to help lovingly guide you through your inner work too, with a focus on spirituality and the Law of Attraction.

So how does healing or inner work connect to love? Well, just like with any form of manifestation, if we have limiting beliefs, fears or trauma standing in our way this acts as an energetic block that stops the Universe from delivering our desires – whether that be love, money, friends, a career or a house, for example. Any blocks or limiting beliefs that may be there under the surface are affecting your Law of Attraction journey and that's why I'm so passionate about sharing this book with you now. I want us all to learn how to embody unconditional love, but in order to do this we must know how to identify and release anything that blocks the path. Which is where my three-step process of *Hurt, Healing, Healed* comes in: to help you identify your own blocks and help you heal and release these through inner work. The quickest way through is by shining love on your limiting beliefs, fears and trauma – and in this book I'll be showing you how to do just that.

The Tools in This Book

Since going through my spiritual awakening in 2016, I found out very quickly along my Law of Attraction journey that the tools and methods I had learned were only going to get me so far in helping me manifest what I wanted in my life. Things would manifest, of course, and with ease most of the time, but the things I really and truly wanted were harder. I also manifested tests and embarked on my twin flame journey for three years (a karmic relationship and a divine mirror), which taught me a heck of a lot about myself and revealed exactly where the inner work needed to be done. Now, don't worry – I'm here to simplify that process for you and share the numerous tools and modalities I've learned along the way from both the Universe and from working with incredible souls. Yes, the answers are always within us but a true guru or teacher will always offer that nudge or positive reminder in the right direction to help you find real healing. So that's what this book is designed to do: remind you of your infinite power and strength as a beautiful human being.

This is the deepest book I've written by far and the one that I believe will give you the biggest results. While *Positively Wealthy* is a fun book that encourages you to dip your toes into the pond of inner work, this new book aims to take you much deeper. It's designed to help you uncover your blocks and to help you find true freedom, fulfilment and happiness in your life so that you can manifest effortlessly and experience unconditional love in all of its forms. Yes, to some that may look like a relationship but unconditional love must always start with loving yourself first!

While some of you picking up this book may be very open to the concepts I include in my work, other readers may think this is too far-fetched for them right now. That's why if you're new to the Law of Attraction and spirituality I would highly recommend reading my two books *Spiritual Queen* and *Positively Wealthy* first so that you can grasp what manifesting is all about and experience a fun and exciting way of seeing the Law of Attraction in action. *Spiritual Queen* shows how you can be a Spiritual Queen in every circumstance in your life by taking charge of what you attract into it, while *Positively Wealthy* will guide you through daily manifestation challenges to complete over 33 days. This book, *Hurt, Healing, Healed*, is about the next stage, although I promise to keep it as straightforward as possible. You know me, I'm a very practical and to-the-point Virgo. I make all of my work easy to understand and accessible because spirituality is for everyone – not a select few. I'm a big believer in incorporating the spiritual, practical and cognitive elements into all that I do with manifesting and healing work, so that's exactly what you can expect within this book. A combination of all three to help you with all aspects of uncovering the blocks in your life and healing them with inner work.

Over the last few years I've been through a lot of healing on all three levels and in order to truly embody that healing I had to incorporate a range of spiritual, practical and cognitive practices. Meditation is an incredible tool and one I swear by. But meditation and manifesting alone will not help you to truly embody healing and experience release. They will work up to a certain level, but from my own experience and those of my clients I can tell you that the same trigger or block will resurface later on – which is probably what led you to pick up this book in the first place! That's why you will find a range of my tools and practices within these pages.

A Little Bit About Me

So, what makes me qualified to share this book with you? Well, during the years that I have worked as an award-winning life coach and mentor, not only have I picked up so many valuable tools, tips and lessons from my own spiritual journey, I have also studied and qualified as an emotional healing coach, Reiki master, EFT (Emotional Freedom Technique) and inner child work practitioner to deepen my work and be able to serve my clients and you all in the best way possible. I have worked with hundreds of thousands of people around the globe to help them transform their lives and manifest abundance through healing.

By the end of this book, you will have learned my three-step process for the stages of *Hurt, Healing, Healed* and the tools and modalities any Spiritual Queen needs to uncover to be able to release limiting beliefs, blocks and trauma. And, of course, I'll be setting you some fun tasks and actions at the end of each chapter so that you have some practical things to go away and implement.

Think of me as your pocket emotional coach over the duration of this book, cheering you on and helping you to remember just how worthy and amazing you truly are. The most exciting part? The fact you get to meet the new you after this process, a you who doesn't operate from fears, negative beliefs or trauma anymore – and meeting that new version of yourself is a very exciting thought!

Manifestation and Privilege

Before we get started, I would like to touch briefly upon manifesting and privilege. While I can only speak as a white, cis, able-bodied woman who is aware of her privilege in life, I do believe the Universe isn't inherently oppressive; it's us as humans with our society and conditioning who have created the many problems such as racism and discrimination against minorities. The Universe is love, remember, and only love. While I know the tools and modalities within this book absolutely work, I also recognize there are other factors involved if you are from the black, people of colour, trans, gender fluid or disabled communities. The results such individuals will get from this book will differ from mine, for example, and may be impacted by the many complexities and oppressive systems that these communities have to face on a daily basis. Having gender fluid and disabled friends in my life, it's really important to me that the manifestation and spiritual space recognize and highlight why different people will get different results with this work and why trauma and healing may differ from community to community.

I don't feel that I'm qualified to talk at length about such important topics, but I can highly recommend checking out the work of playwright and producer Trey Anthony, a beautiful black woman whose work I adore and who offers insightful perspectives on issues such as diversity and inclusivity in the spirituality and wellbeing spheres. Another great resource on diversity in the wellbeing industry is a great platform called thy.self, which has a wealth of resources and content for you to explore on diversity in the wellbeing industry. I hope and pray that as great movements such as Black Lives Matter continue to bring awareness of these issues to the forefront, black people, people of colour, trans, gender fluid and disabled people will all experience a life of ease and equality in all forms of abundance too.

Your Three-Step Process to Healing

The main focus of *Hurt, Healing, Healed* is all around your mindset and manifestation. So many people ask me how to shift their mindset that I wanted to create a formula and process that helps you successfully do just that! This book is divided into three parts that deal with the three main levels of healing, as shown in the diagram below.

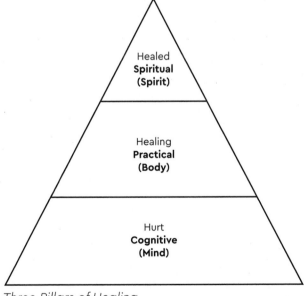

Three Pillars of Healing

Now that you can see my three pillars of healing in the diagram, I want to break this down into my step-by-step process for achieving the ultimate outcome of healing. These steps are all incorporated in each section of this book to give you the best results.

Hurt – Cognitive (Mind)

Meaning: betrayal, disconnected from unconditional love, confusion, loss, pain, numbness, seeking, longing, avoidance.

First of all we need to work with the mind to identify any blocks, resistance, fears, beliefs and trauma that could be blocking you currently. This is done by exploring the conscious and subconscious mind safely and reprogramming your core beliefs into new positive beliefs. Awareness is key in this cognitive stage and I will explore your mindset with you and help you to create a positive abundant mindset.

Healing – Practical (Body)

Meaning: on the journey back to love, remembering love and Source, process that is evolving and changing constantly, moving toward connection, liminal stage, movement, chrysalis transforming, transformation process, feeling shifts, tears, release, awareness, forgiveness, self-acceptance, surrender, flow.

In this second stage we explore the practical steps to healing through physical activities, exercises and energy stored in your physical and energetic body. This step is all about taking action toward releasing the past and healing your emotional body.

Healed – Spiritual (Spirit)

Meaning: flourishing, blossoming, reconnecting, shine, light, expansive, connected to unconditional love, peace, empowered, abundance, clarity, ease, receive, reveal, trust, belief, warmth.

Finally, we work with the spiritual side of things to bring all of this together through integration. As much as we need to consider the human mind and body, we also need to energetically release and heal through our spiritual side. This step looks at the merging of your human self with the metaphysical side of healing to bring you back into alignment with yourself and Source (another name for the Universe).

How to Work with This Book

This is a book for anyone who feels reactive, angry, triggered, unsafe, rageful, controlling or freaks out when things are out of their control. In the next few chapters, I'll go through the key signs that limiting beliefs and fears are present, but if you feel triggered and irritable in your daily life then this is the book for you. This book is also for you if you lack confidence, if you procrastinate, if you experience perfectionism, lack of self-worth, lack of belief or have any negative feelings at all for that matter. *Hurt, Healing, Healed* has been designed to help you feel peace within yourself again and come into true alignment with your desires.

Throughout the book there are lots of practical tasks and actions at the end of each chapter to summarize and help you along this process, and I would suggest dedicating a special notebook to your *Hurt, Healing, Healed* journey so that all your reflections and notes are safe in one place.

The book has been written in a specific order to guide you along the healing journey, so you may want to read the entire thing first in a linear order and then come back to individual chapters to give them your full energy at a later date. The most important part is that you don't skip any of the steps. You can absolutely take it at your own pace but by following the structure of the book you'll see big shifts and changes by the end as I cover each step of the process thoroughly.

I hope you're ready for some awesome inner work, Queen, because while it's going to be a journey it will be one of the most rewarding adventures of your life. I can vouch for this wholeheartedly. I wouldn't be who I am today without having been on this deep inner journey. Your future self who has these desires you wish for is already thanking you for picking up this book and dedicating the time to this work. You deserve healing, Queen, and you deserve a life full of beauty, magic and abundance. Remember, everything is energy, so when we clear the way to abundance there is nothing in this world that can stop our desires from manifesting. So affirm that today and know the life you truly want is awaiting you.

The Law of Attraction and Healing

You may already be aware of the inner (shadow) work that comes up with a spiritual or Law of Attraction journey, or you may be a complete newbie and thinking, "Hey Emma, what's blocking my manifestations?" About a year or so into my spiritual journey was when my real, deep shadow work came up to the surface. That's not to say I didn't experience inner work before then, but it certainly deepened when I went on my twin flame journey.

Essentially, the Law of Attraction is one of the seven laws of the Universe; it's the belief that we can attract anything we want into our lives. It's all about having a positive and grateful mindset and being conscious that if we can see something in our mind, we can hold it in our hands. Like attracts like.

"A bit like karma" is the best way I can explain the Law of Attraction. What you put out into the world you get back. For example, if you're being loving, kind, caring and happy, you're going to attract lots of incredible miracles into your life, including more love. But if you're being negative, expecting the worst to happen and doubting everything – then guess what? Your life isn't going to look too positive.

The Law of Attraction also teaches us that we are constantly speaking and thinking things into existence – so wherever your energy goes, it will manifest into your reality. The Universe matches our energy, so essentially we get what we tolerate in life.

The Five Steps of the Law of Attraction

After learning about the Law of Attraction, I realized that there are more than just the usual three steps (these being Ask, Believe and Receive) and so I developed these into the following five channelled steps in my first book, *Spiritual Queen*:

1. Ask

The first and most important step in the Law of Attraction is to ask the Universe, God, Source, Divine – whatever it is you connect with – for what you desire. It's really important to know exactly what you want and to be specific. Don't worry if you have absolutely no idea right now what it is you want in life; the Universe will soon help you out along the way. I always find that focusing on things that bring me joy is a great way to establish what I want. You don't have to manifest materialistic things. You can manifest emotions, answers and guidance galore! You can even manifest to be shown what your next step should be. The way to ask the Universe can be as simple as saying it out loud – for example, "Universe, I would like to manifest my monthly salary increasing." I always like to add the words "and so it is" at the end in order to see it as done. Whether you keep a goals list, say your manifestation verbally, write it down as an affirmation, think it or put it on a vision board, these are *all* ways of asking, and you only need to ask once.

2. Believe

The second step is to believe that your desire will manifest at the perfect time. Now, I know some of you will be saying, "Well, I just asked – so how come my money, dream career and hunky husband aren't knocking at my door?!" The answer is divine timing. The Universe has a set timeline for you, and everything will manifest at exactly the right time. Enjoy that process too. It's no fun if you get everything at once – if that happened, what would you focus on manifesting? If you find it hard to believe that your desire can be yours, then ask for a sign. Connect to your angels, spirit guides or simply the Universe and ask for a sign that your desire has been heard. Belief can take some time, so make sure that you're doing your daily practices and challenges in this book, where you'll be working on your vibration, energy and self-love in order to be in the best place possible to receive your manifestation.

3. Trust

This is an important step that I've added into the manifestation process. This is very similar to the Believe step earlier, but I do think the two are separate. There will be a period where you're waiting for your manifestation to appear. This is when it's vital to trust the Universe's plan and find inner peace with the outcome. Essentially, this means acting as if you already have your desire. For example, if you want to manifest your dream partner, you would date yourself, commit to yourself, take inspired action and love yourself. After all, if you had your dream partner you would be relaxed, feeling loved and getting on with your life. You wouldn't be sitting indoors waiting on a text or feeling miserable. So really connect to the feelings you would have if your heart's desire were here right now, and live them now!

4. Let Go

This fourth step is arguably one of the most important and another one that I've added to the usual trio of Ask, Believe and Receive. Although letting go is a vital part of the manifestation process, for some reason most Law of Attraction methods skip past it. Let it all go – though it may seem confusing that you should ask for your desire and then forget all about it, right? Crazy, I know, but you actually make things happen so much faster when you let go. Letting go means that you're totally okay with either outcome. If you want or need something so much that you get desperate about it, then you're putting out a vibe of lack, and just like karma, that's what you're going to attract back: lack. Believing that your desire will manifest, while at the same time being really grateful for what you have now and accepting the possibility of a different outcome, is an absolute game-changer. This is the miracle: seeing how far you've come, honouring your growth and not even needing the manifestation anymore. You still hold that manifestation as your end goal, but you release how and when it will happen. By doing this you attract your desire so much faster; and by living in the now, having fun and focusing on other things, you let the Universe get to work!

5. Receive

This is the final step: receiving your manifestation. YASS! Now let the partying begin. You may receive signs, numbers or even snippets of intuition that your manifestation is on the way. I often sense something the day before it happens. If you do, just relax and get excited, baby! Honour your journey, thank the Universe and be grateful that your desire has been delivered to you.

Doing the Inner Work

The number one problem many run into with manifesting is hitting blocks and limiting beliefs. Many think they can bypass these with "positivity" and it's okay, Queen, we've all done this because that is what we're told to do in many old-school Law of Attraction books. Just think happy positive thoughts and nothing else matters! Well, how's that been working out for you? Probably, like for me, not so great with those negative thoughts and fears still sat there, never moving or releasing, no matter how much we try to fake it until we make it!

We didn't know any better at the time, and it's only when we're brought to our knees by the Universe that we realize the only way out is through – and these things are coming up for a reason. This is the work many don't speak about on the spiritual journey – and it is a journey, remember. You don't just spiritually awaken and then that's it – every desire is yours! Yes, of course, manifestations and desires will come to you, but everyone is different and unique and that means their inner work will be too.

I've always tried to include the inner work in my books and methods as I realized the importance of this in order to welcome in your manifestations and abundance. With all my big manifestations I've had to clear resistance, limiting beliefs or fears, and work on things like worth, self-love and even past lives too! But where is this spoken about in the usual Law of Attraction process? Many teachers and authors are starting to mention the importance of this work more often, but not in the sense of offering an accessible guide on how to identify these blocks and then release them. Now, I am a big advocate for working with professionals in a safe space to identify and release these in a safe way, and I've worked with numerous spiritual and cognitive therapists myself over the years. However, as with all my work, I want to make this process accessible for people who aren't able to afford coaching or who want to dive into this journey by themselves as long as it's safe to do so. Remember that the power is always within you and all that any spiritual teacher or coach is ever really doing is reminding you of your innate power.

The reason why this work is so important and why I felt the need to write a whole book on this subject is because we need this as a collective now more than ever. Many give up with the Law of Attraction or feel abundance isn't for them because of the inner work involved. Some paint the Law of Attraction as this easy journey to abundance but don't share the full picture with us. We need the full scope of the spiritual journey and its essence to understand all the laws of the Universe and how integrating all of these is how we actually manifest our desires. This lack of information is why many people think they're doing it wrong or don't believe the Law of Attraction works for them. It breaks my heart to hear or see this because *everyone* is worthy and deserving of abundance and it is possible for everyone. It's not just for a select few or the Law of Attraction experts you see online.

This is the missing key in any Spiritual Queen's toolkit, because when you can clear the way of blocks and resistance you become a magnet for abundance. When you clear anything holding you back or keeping you small in life, you step more into your authentic self, which allows you to align with your greatest desires. This is all about vibration, your energy and aligning yourself to your truest version who has these desires.

It is my hope and aim for this book that more and more people DO believe in themselves, DO manifest their dreams and DO see success. Many make out the Law of Attraction to be a super-easy process, and while I'm all for affirming it's easy, of course it's a little more complex than that. What about when irrational thoughts and fears are plaguing us? What if we don't feel worthy? What if we're resisting change?

Healing and the Law of Attraction

Healing and releasing are an essential part of the Law of Attraction. You may have heard about the concept of creating space in your life for your desires before. But truly making space means at a mental, emotional and physical level. You have to work on all three levels for the space to be truly created. While it's great to declutter your home and clothes, etc., you have to declutter your mind and emotions of any stagnant or negative energy too – and that's what we're going to do in this book.

So what causes blocks and limiting beliefs? Well, life! We live in a very busy world where we don't always get things right. We're learning on the job, and we arrive here having agreed to soul contracts that determine some of our lessons in this life. We also have ancestral trauma travelling down our family lines too. So, it makes for a nice little spiritual cocktail – and it's now time for our generation and lifetime to help heal these for good and stop ancestral trauma, for example, from going any further.

Think about it: if we were taught about mindfulness and spirituality in school, imagine how differently we would experience life? Now, everything does happen for a reason and it's important to remember there is no blame involved here either for yourself or others. I know that may be triggering to read for some people, especially those who have experienced abuse, so trust that as this book unfolds you may be able to lean into this a little more.

As you dive deeper into this book, certain things may come up for you and it's important you honour these. This book is your guide to help with those triggers and emotions that may be coming up for you. Witness, allow and release these in your own time. Healing is not linear and that's one thing I want to make clear from the get-go. If you think this journey will be a straight "a to b, job's a good-un", you may be disappointed. The one thing I've learned over my healing journey is that it takes time, commitment and surrender.

You may finish this book and then feel great and experience six months of joy, abundance and manifestations. Then you may find something else comes up and you need to pick up this book again. This is all part of our cyclical nature and how the rhythms of life work. It's not that you're not doing the work or that it hasn't worked. Think of healing as being a little like an onion, and you're peeling away the layers with inner work; so each time something comes up in the future or you feel triggered, it will become less and less intense. I always say judge your comeback rate, not the thoughts and emotions that come up. If you feel able to pull yourself back into a neutral space of peace quicker each time, then you know the process is working. This again highlights that nobody can predict a healing journey so something might release quite quickly for good or you may have a few layers come up over a period of time.

While some of the concepts and tools in this book may not be everyone's cup of tea, embrace what you can. I ask you to have an open heart, open mind and open approach to your healing journey. I also think there's a lot of emphasis on what is meant by a "healing journey", which may seem heavy or a lot for some people. A healing journey is basically your spiritual journey – you may only have a few things to shift or you may have years to unpack. If you only have a few things to work through that don't feel major to you, don't worry – honour this. Remember this is a journey of ebbing and flowing; in fact, you may just read this book and not need to use any of the tools or modalities right now – celebrate this too. Do what feels good and come back to anything else that doesn't. Healing doesn't just have to be for spiritual folk. Healing is for everyone and, as always, I try to keep things as accessible and easy to understand as possible.

Healing to me means returning to my true self, the person I came here to be. It means unpacking any of the unnecessary baggage I've picked up in this lifetime that isn't mine to carry and for the stuff that is, working to lovingly release this. It means clearing the way for happiness, joy, abundance and returning to unconditional love. Healing to me means coming home to myself fully and feeling peace and love in my soul and body.

Ask yourself this or maybe even journal upon this: *What does healing mean to me?* Healing doesn't mean you're broken, faulty or that you need to be fixed – because that would be the case for every single human being if it were true! We all have weights we're carrying around – some that are visible and some that aren't – so it's important we reframe what healing looks like and help people to know asking for support or help is brave, it's courageous and it's *not* a form of weakness, ever.

Different Healing Journeys

Doing the inner work has transformed my life in so many ways. It has allowed me to experience pure bliss and happiness, and manifest the most beautiful blessings into my life. It has allowed me to align with and embody my true self and express this into the world. It has allowed me to return home to myself finally. But this isn't just about me; there are so many incredible real life stories out there just like mine. And that is why I want to share with you the experiences and results of some of my spiritual peers and coaching clients who have undergone their own healing journey ...

"My transformation journey required a lot of letting go, slowing down and self-love. Having been a CEO of a tech company for a number of years I had spent a lot of time in my masculine energy in a male-dominated environment, so the most important inner work that I had to do involved embracing my feminine, which included meditations, forgiveness and learning to nurture myself.

The inner work I have done has been the most important thing in my life, it has helped me to understand what matters most to me and to give time and energy to those people and activities. In addition to meditations to help me step into my feminine, I now have a strong gratitude practice and I have found EFT (Emotional Freedom Technique) to be the most effective practice for changing the way I feel when anxiety or overwhelms sets in. Writing and journaling have also been fundamental to my progress. My life is now on my terms, I have freed myself from toxicity in my working life and I stand strong when it comes to protecting my boundaries. By doing this I attract the people and projects that work best for me."

Dr Becky Sage, Life and Business coaching client

"Inner work itself is the most important thing in any transformation or change in life. If I didn't do my own work around my beliefs and mindset I wouldn't be able to be where I am now. When we work on inner healing, we work on ourselves to have a better, happier, healthier and abundant life. I love to do my inner healing with journaling, affirmations, coaching, memberships group, gratitude list and meditations. Now after a long and very rewarding inner work journey my life is so different. I run my own business, my self-confidence is bursting out of the roof, and my health improvement of 100 per cent (lost all pain, lost weight, low moods gone etc.). Inner work was and still is a very important part of my life."

Michaela Hornakova, Life and Business coaching client

"In the past I struggled with self-belief. I thought that my own feelings and beliefs were alien. I feared I was an outcast who had no place rejecting what I felt was not for me. For example, I had a strong sense from a young age that having children wasn't for me. However, I was surrounded by a world that kept telling me I was going to make a wonderful mother and there was no greater joy or purpose than bearing a child. So much so I started to walk a path every bone in my body was telling me was wrong, just to be what everyone around me told me I should be, as I had no confidence in myself.

Having done the inner work, I discovered that not wanting children didn't mean I was worth any less than others. That there is nothing wrong with me or who I am. I wouldn't be the strong, independent, confident woman I am now without it. If I hadn't done the work I would still be letting the doubt in myself allow me to walk paths others tell me I should instead of following my own truth. Healing my lack of self-belief has not only helped me with this, but in every area of my life. I can make decisions with certainty. I know I can trust myself and know who I am. My life now is so much more positive. I have attracted true friends who accept all of me. I am able to navigate conversations and communicate at a whole new level. I have also been able to set and stick to healthy boundaries."

Amber Perman, Spiritual Queen in my community

"For me, the inner work has been fundamental in helping me reclaim my inner peace and sense of empowerment and wellbeing. That no matter what I go through, I can ride the storm with grace and temperance.

An example of this was embarking on a hypnotherapy journey that led me to past-life regression. The combination of these two things enabled me to begin inner child healing but also to reclaim lost parts of myself that I hadn't even realized I had suppressed through addictive behaviour patterns that weren't helping my mental state with the health situation I was in. I was able to release these addictive patterns, which brought me a whole new sense of freedom. The outcome of this was that it started helping to heal my mental health and bring me to a more peaceful state of mind, allowing me to deal with my health situation and to feel stronger, more empowered and in control of my life again. With the aftercare of this treatment I learned specific visualization, autogenic imagery and self-hypnosis techniques. This also led to a deeper meditation practice and brought me to a much more consistent place with my self-care and overall wellbeing."

Hannah Wallace, writer and speaker

"Like many people, the lockdown brought up deep-seated, unresolved traumas that I had to deal with. Inundated by triggers I couldn't understand and overwhelmed with emotions I couldn't release with my existing healing tools and modalities, I knew I had to ask for external help. Often, we think that just because we're spiritual or we teach about healing, we have to be happy 24/7 or know how to resolve what we're going through without external help. In truth, we need to keep it real and realize that human emotion is nothing to feel guilty about, and asking for help is a sign of courage rather than weakness. I was inspired to work with Kamran Bedi, an Integral Eye Movement Therapy (IEMT) coach. In just four sessions I was able to heal traumas and limiting beliefs I'd been struggling to release for years. Doing the inner work has allowed me to follow my purpose and improve my quality of life in every respect. Healing past hurts and limiting beliefs has allowed me to trust in myself more, develop my gifts and abilities, and show up confidently in my work and relationships."

George Lizos, bestselling author and intuitive

I love these empowering, real, raw stories because no matter what inner work may be coming up for you, healing and abundance are possible. You've got this, Queen, you always had – and this book is a reminder to come home to yourself to feel ease and peace once again. Are you ready to welcome in true unconditional love and abundance again? Then let's begin ...

PART ONE:
Hurt

"It is our wounds that create in us a desire to reach for miracles."

Jocelyn Soriano, *Mend My Broken Heart*

In this section I will explore with you what causes hurt, the layers to this and how you can start to identify the inner work that needs to be done. I will lovingly guide you through the process of uncovering your hurt and help you understand what blocks you from manifesting your desires currently. By the end of Part One, you will be ready to do the inner work, have awareness of your pain, have the courage to move forward and be prepared to transform your pain into healing.

What Causes Limiting Beliefs and Fears?

Think back to your childhood – to all the magic and wonder that surrounded you as a child. I now want you to revisit memories or defining moments when that same magic felt lost and the harsh reality of this Earth started to set in. When unconditional love suddenly felt conditional and the dream began to disappear.

As children we're born into this world pure beings of unconditional love; we witness this when a baby is born and the pure love that we feel toward these perfect bundles of joy. As that baby begins to grow and experience this world, they start to pick up on their surroundings. The toddler develops into a child and absorbs even more of their environment; the magic starts to feel clouded and they become conditioned by all they're absorbing and learning. By the age of seven the child has formulated all their core beliefs and mental patterns and starts to display this through their personality and actions.

You may be wondering how this relates to your manifestation journey or even to yourself as an adult. See, the thing is, within us all there is a version of ourselves who is still running the show in the form of our inner child. I believe the inner child disguises themselves as our inner critic and ego; so that doubtful nagging voice in your mind that holds you back, puts you down and is worried about everything you do is really just another version of yourself. The inner child will appear to everyone at a different age, but they are there waiting for us to acknowledge and love them. (We will cover more of this later on, in Part Two.)

The good news is that as well as the inner child we also have a higher self – our love and light self. The higher self is part of our spirit team, which is designed to guide and teach us in this lifetime and we can always reach out for support from them. And then we have our human self – the you who is reading this book now. But for now, let's get to know our inner child.

When I explain the spiritual side of manifesting, I always include the inner child because it's such an important factor when looking at where those belief systems and fears stem from that block us from manifesting. Now, as we know from the previous chapter, everything is energy – but emotions are energy in motion and if you have trapped emotions in your body, for example, or you have some negative core beliefs, all of this *is* affecting your manifestations and how you feel within yourself. So how do we get limiting beliefs or fears?

Limiting beliefs come from accepting that something about ourselves, others or the world is true and are the result of the different things that happen to us in our lives. Many of our limiting beliefs develop in childhood when we aren't so well equipped to process what is happening to us. Childhood trauma can come in the form of many things, including abuse (physical and emotional), neglect, abandonment, tragic events, enmeshment (such as having parents with no personal boundaries) or a lack of approval, affection and affirmation. When something traumatic happens, the feelings from that moment can remain stuck in your subconscious mind, causing you to replay this memory over and over again whenever your subconscious perceives the same threat.

When I first dived into this work, I thought there was no way I'd experienced trauma as a child because I had a good upbringing, but as I looked at the above description of childhood trauma, as explained by popular psychologists, I realized many of us experience these traumatic events and don't even realize how much of an impact they have on our lives.

Often, limiting beliefs are unconscious thoughts that act as a defence mechanism to help us avoid possible negative experiences or emotions, such as frustration, anxiety, anger or sadness, for example. These beliefs are often triggered by specific memories that may have hurt you in the past. So your subconscious tries to block these new experiences by altering your thoughts and behaviour, which can result in negative outcomes like procrastination, conformism, overthinking, anxiety or impostor syndrome, to name a few.

Dr Bruce Lipton, author of the bestselling book *The Biology of Belief*, talks about how from birth to around age seven, we operate primarily in brain wavelengths that are very close to a hypnotic state. You see, as children we're literally like sponges, absorbing everything around us from our caregivers, parents and family members. To show you an example of how this plays out in your life, think about your parents' or caregivers' relationship with money: how would you describe it? Now, what is your relationship with money and who do you resemble? When I asked this in a money masterclass, all of the Queens who attended were shocked at how accurate this observation is. Money is one example but we could also apply this to love, friendships, body image or whatever – we are all products of our environment, growing up.

As well as this, there is a spiritual factor that comes into play when we develop limiting beliefs or fears, and that is ancestral trauma. We can inherit limiting beliefs, fear and trauma that are passed down through the generations of our father and mother (paternal and maternal) lines. This could be from only a few generations back or even date back to centuries ago. After doing Family Constellation sessions (which are therapeutic sessions that help reveal the hidden dynamics in families) during the process of writing this book to heal my mother line, I realized that some of my core fears and patterns, such as a fear of safety with men, were never really mine to start with, yet I can remember having this fear for as long as I remember. When diving into this, I discovered the fear actually came from a relative far back along my mother line and it was being passed on from one generation to the next.

This is why your work here is so important, because when you do the healing work you're not just doing it for yourself – you're doing it for your relatives, ancestors and future lines too. This is powerful stuff, meaning that our children and future generations won't repeat these patterns or have to experience what we or our ancestors have experienced.

You can also bring limiting beliefs, fears and trauma through from your past lives. I worked with a client who had an irrational fear of getting on planes; she had tried every healing modality going and yet still she couldn't even go to the airport. I suggested working with a past-life regression expert to explore this as I couldn't find any trauma in this lifetime that correlated to this deep fear of hers. Finally, after doing a past-life regression session, she got her answers, cleared the fear and started to build up to getting on a plane again.

And Now for the Science ...

As neuroscience isn't my field of expertise, I invited expert brain re-wirer and coach Bob Doyle to explain how limiting beliefs and fears work from a biological and science perspective. Bob's work is featured in Rhonda Byrne's book and movie *The Secret*. He told me:

> "In my 20 years of teaching the Law of Attraction, the topic of "limiting beliefs" has always been at the top of the list as to the reason people are slower to manifest than they'd like. In my teaching and coaching, I would talk about the energetic resistance that these beliefs would create in terms of moving one's self into vibrational alignment with their vision. The "frequency" of the resistance caused by the limiting beliefs literally resists, or pushes away, anything that is vibrating in alignment with the actual receiving of the goal.
>
> While all of those ideas would definitely fall into the "metaphysical" category, let's look at what's happening on a biological level and what's happening here on the physcial plane.
>
> Our beliefs determine to a great extent the action we will or won't take in our lives. And because most manifestations are a direct or indirect result of action we take, our beliefs play a crucial role in our manifestation success.
>
> At a biological level, beliefs are determined by how our brains are wired, or programmed, over the course of our lifetime. In fact, our wiring runs the entire show. Taking a look at how we are wired, and how we can change that wiring, becomes very valuable when it comes to manifesting with intention.
>
> From about age zero to seven, our brains are wide open and ready to receive. Before our brain is developed enough for us to have our own capabilities for critical

thinking, we basically are saying "yes" to all the input from the outside world. If our parents have limiting beliefs about money, then we are very likely to be programmed with those same beliefs and act accordingly throughout our lives. The action we take is very likely to reinforce these beliefs that have been wired, and thus we get the appropriate results based on that action – whether we want that result or not.

The power comes from knowing that although our brains are not as "plastic" as they were when we first came into this world, we still have the ability to change any wiring in our brain that is not serving us. However, in order for us to change that wiring so that our "default" behaviour can actually sustain new results, we must re-teach the brain.

Instead of allowing our deeply wired, auto-pilot responses to determine the action we take, we need to learn to become aware of those responses and consciously change them on an ongoing basis in order for new neural pathways to be formed to support a "new normal."

The challenge with simply changing our autopilot responses is that when we have an emotional reaction to something – large or small – our body produces a flood of chemicals based on thoughts and feelings that are triggered in a situation. We are literally under the influence of our own drugs. Exactly what reaction occurs depends fully on your brain's wiring, and how it is processing the details of the moment. Depending on the situation, this change in body chemistry can feel great, terrible or something in-between. When our body chemistry takes over, it's even more difficult to override our auto-pilot reactions, despite the fact that we realize that we're experiencing pre-wired behaviour.

The reason so many people do not ultimately have success with the Law of Attraction or manifesting in general, is that they do not send new thoughts and ideas to their brains consistently enough for the new wiring to take hold. Most people stop way too soon, with the idea that if the thing hasn't manifested yet, then "the Universe doesn't want it" for them, or that they are going against the flow, so they stop ... which only reinforces the older, default wiring.

However, if one has the support and/or proper inspiration to become aware of, stop and change their autopilot responses, then the resulting new action that occurs puts new energetic events into place, and this is where the Law of Attraction does its thing, pulling in the circumstances to which we must react.

It is how we react that determines what the Universe does next. It is only when we become aware of how our wiring unconsciously controls us that we can truly become intentional manifestors on a consistent and more predictable basis."

You can find out more about Bob Doyle's work at his website meetbobdoyle.com.

Another interesting perspective comes from Dr Bruce D Perry, an American psychiatrist who wrote a book with Oprah Winfrey called *What Happened to You?* (a great read if this work fascinates you like it does me). In the book, they explain that we shouldn't ask people "Why are you like that?" but instead ask "What happened to you?" I feel deeply this is an important question we should all ask ourselves. When you realize that everyone is merely acting from that small childlike version of themselves who went through certain experiences, you begin to realize nothing is ever really just about you – it's always about the other person too and how they feel about themselves and their core beliefs.

So we've covered how core beliefs are formed and where they stem from – but is it possible to get more of these beliefs once we are over seven years old? Absolutely! We can still experience new fears, beliefs and trauma at any age, but what I have found in my own healing and with clients is that what we think is a "happened at 15 years old" problem nearly always stems back to the core beliefs we had as a child. Now, as we do the work in this book, not everyone will go as far back as age seven or younger but it is very likely and usual to do so. What you normally find is that you'll remember a key event or feeling in your teenage years but actually you first would have felt the core feelings or emotions much younger. In our adult years we can then start to make limiting decisions that trigger our core limiting beliefs – it always starts with a limiting decision first, which leads to the core belief being reaffirmed in our subconscious.

The Link Between Love and Fear

Love and fear are the only two things we can experience, and yet we can't feel both of them at the same time. But we can feel these emotions very closely to one another; for example, when experiencing desire or even entering into a new relationship we can feel deep love and then fear can follow very closely behind it – this is a sign that the inner child is at play and there is some inner work that needs to be done.

So how is it that we can experience pure moments of joy and happiness and then feel an overwhelming sense of fear? Well, sometimes getting what we want *is* scary because it triggers a version of ourselves who has experienced loss; you may have felt this yourself before and, while any belief could be playing out here, the fear comes from the inner child screaming out for reassurance and wanting to know it's safe to let their guard down again and unconditionally love something. Loving anything unconditionally is scary for a wounded inner child, as seeing something so pure and amazing only reminds of us experiencing that loss of magic and wonder in ourselves as a child – and that's why this work is so important. So that we can love ourselves and others openly, unconditionally and from a trusting space.

It's very easy when reading all of this information to spiral into a place of shame and judgement. Believe me, no one is perfect and as humans we are all traumatized in our own way. As weighty as that term is to use, we are all hurt in some way and are experiencing different versions of that. We learn these belief systems as a child and then move through life creating experiences that match our beliefs.

The good news is that because we can't feel love and fear at the same time, whenever we are feeling moments of fear and anxiety, evoking feelings of love will help us return to a natural, peaceful place.

Why Do We Have Fears and Shame?

So why do we all have limiting beliefs, fears and trauma? Well, from a spiritual point of view we came to Earth to learn in the classroom of life. We pick upbringings, scenarios and circumstances that give us the opportunity to learn and support our soul's evolution. Essentially, as I mentioned at the start of this chapter, we are all born into this world as pure beings of unconditional love, but life and society teach us how to disconnect from this and experience hurt. It's then our job to remove the barriers along our journey and come back home to ourselves and unconditional love.

One example of how society plays a large part in our conditioning and how we the view the world is made clear when women discuss pleasure and sex. I use this example as it's a topic that my friends and I have discussed at great depth, including why we've felt shame in bringing it up.

For thousands of years women have experienced suppression in society for everything from their periods to sexual pleasure and even for initiating sex; so when my friend asked me once why she couldn't initiate sex or why she felt shame around these subjects I reminded her that, yes, some of it could be linked to her past – but all women feel this too because of societal conditioning. We have been conditioned to feel shame and judgement around many of these issues so it's great to see in my adulthood that women are starting to reclaim their power and rewrite the story and beliefs around sexuality.

I want you to look at your childhood, upbringing, experiences and conditioning without shame and judgement. This is a judgement-free zone and it's about looking beyond what's wrong or right because, really, who are we to judge that?

It's important to remember our parents and caregivers were doing the best they could for us with what they knew. At the same time, it's also important to acknowledge any abuse a child has been through from a parent and recognize how that child's parent may have been acting out of their own hurt and experiences. This goes for everyone: we're all doing the best we can with the tools and awareness we have at that time.

Ways Our Fears and Beliefs Play Out

Some other ways that limiting beliefs, fears and trauma play out is in our relationships. Our divine assignments (by this, I mean our key relationships such as with soulmates, karmic connections and twin flames, etc.) will be the biggest triggers of our inner work as they reflect to us the lessons and wounds that need to be looked at.

I myself felt very codependent in relationships for many years, which stemmed from my own relationship with my parents when I was growing up and how this taught me what love should look and feel like. I went for emotionally unavailable men to suppress my deep ancestral fear and my own fear of commitment. Although commitment was actually the very thing I was seeking, underneath all of that lay my own fear of commitment – and the emotionally unavailable men were reflecting this fear and energy back to me.

Through doing the inner work I learned to be independent and love myself. I was able to provide for myself and be okay by myself without validation from men, which was transformative for me in so many ways. I'm now in a healthy relationship where we are both independent people who choose to meet in the middle and can coexist as a team without either depending on the other in an unbalanced way.

Equally, someone who is extremely independent might not let in anyone else or allow themselves to be held. They may fear commitment for the same reasons as I did, but that may manifest as being an overly independent person who prefers their own company and can't commit.

Ideally, we want to be well balanced and self-dependent in our relationships. That way, we allow people in and let ourselves be supported, but at the same time, we don't become needy and rely on another person for our happiness as that's how we always end up losing ourselves.

As you can see, there are a whole array of limiting beliefs and fears that we can experience, but the most common limiting belief that I come across, and which many women I work with have but which also affects men, is around self-worth – and not feeling worthy or enough. I have had to work on this a lot during my spiritual journey too, and I may just attract this type of person to my work because I've experienced and healed this in myself.

So how do we identify what limiting beliefs and fears are in our subconscious? You may be consciously aware of what limiting beliefs you have playing out in your life already, and you may have even had some breakthroughs and realizations from reading this chapter so far. But some do go under the radar in the subconscious and it's my job throughout this book to help you safely uncover these.

Most people have between 60,000 and 80,000 thoughts a day. Imagine if every thought we perceived about ourselves and our world were true? Subconsciously, you already disregard a lot of the thoughts that enter your mind. The next step is to identify the negative thoughts that do not serve you and examine them closely. By understanding the core fear or emotion behind our limiting beliefs, we can then begin to heal these and let these damaging thoughts peacefully leave us.

Too often we judge the thoughts that come into our heads and worry that we're being too negative or that we've had a bad or a shameful thought. But when we witness these without judgement as just thoughts and part of us, the force they hold instantly dissolves and we take back our power.

Fear and Trauma in the Body

I like to think of trauma as being an unloved aspect of ourselves that we need to love back into integration. Instead of rejecting our trauma or seeing it as negative, we need to move toward it, embrace it and tell it that it's okay. Remember that your inner child is at the root of all of this – so love, compassion and embracing them is exactly what your fears and trauma need right now.

It may seem like an exciting task to work through all your limiting beliefs or it may even seem scary and triggering. That's why it's important to go slow with this process and only look at one or two blocks at a time. (You can always come back once you're ready to work on another belief.) There are many benefits to this approach, as it means the process doesn't become too overwhelming and it ensures that you give each belief the energy and focus it needs to properly clear and release.

The best way I've found to start this journey is to begin with the most prominent belief or fear holding you back. To find out what this is, think about your desires and one in particular you've really struggled with manifesting. Now I want you to close your eyes and take a deep breath in and on the exhale just release any stress or tension from your day so far. Next, I would like you to focus on your desire and see yourself with this manifestation. I'm now going to say something and I want you to take note of where on your body you feel something as I say it. Ready?

Your manifestation is not going to happen.

Where on your body did you feel pain, resistance, uncomfortable or uneasy?

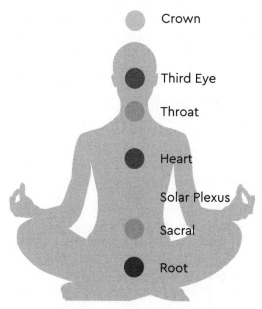

Crown

Third Eye

Throat

Heart

Solar Plexus

Sacral

Root

The location of the seven chakras in the physical body

- Crown – connection to spirituality and the divine (the Universe)
- Third Eye – inner vision, intuition, outer vision (what are you not seeing?)
- Throat – voicing and speaking up or your truth (what are you not voicing or over-voicing?)
- Heart – Giving and receiving unconditional love, how we love
- Solar Plexus – Power, action, confidence
- Sacral – Creativity, sexuality, sensuality and pleasure
- Root – Stability, grounding, foundations

Now let's look at which chakra in your energetic body this part of your body represents. I am bringing in the chakras because these play a key role in our spiritual body and where we store emotions and feelings. If, for instance, you felt a pain in your heart chakra then this is a clue that your core belief relates to giving and receiving love. If the pain was in your throat chakra then the block relates to not being able to speak up, voice your truth or say what you need to say – maybe you're not being honest with yourself?

Identify in which chakra you felt something by using the picture above.

Once you've identified the chakra, I now want you to place a hand over that area on your physical body and tune in to the fear that comes up. What words, feelings or emotions come up as you tune in to this fear? These might be about loss, lack, acceptance or feeling not enough, for example. Trust the words and emotions that are coming up for you and write these down in your notebook or journal.

Finally, I want you to take the core words or emotions from this fear and now place a hand on your heart space (at centre of your chest) and breathe into this space. I would like you to tune in to the fear and your core words and ask yourself, "When was the first time I felt this?" Write down the first number that pops into your mind even if you can't remember what happened at that age. Trust the first age that comes up for you.

So now you have identified your primary limiting belief or fear that is blocking your biggest desire. The reason why we look at this one first is because this will always be the strongest and most potent in your life. From this point on, you can use the tools and stages in this book to work on this and discover more about your belief and where it stems from.

Another great question to ask yourself if your feeling was "I'm not enough" is to enquire into who taught you that. While we won't always be taught every belief we have by someone we know, very often we learn these core emotions and wounds from our parents, caregivers, family and experiences growing up and in school.

As well as in our energetic body and our chakras, limiting beliefs and fears can show up in the physical body. One of my favourite books that has helped me to understand this side of healing is *The Body Keeps the Score* by Bessel Van Der Kolk. It's a very deep, research-based book that is fascinating to read and explains how our body stores our limiting beliefs, fears and trauma. I won't go into too much of the science here, but this aspect is why I work with the practical, cognitive and spiritual sides of healing – because we need all three pillars to truly embody healing and to be able to move forward from a new healed space.

An example of this happened for me a few years ago when I wasn't speaking up or voicing my truth in a situation; so after clearing my throat constantly, the Universe knew it had to step up to get my attention. I then developed laryngitis and couldn't speak for 10 days. With no choice but to slow down and rest, I had time to address the situation I wasn't speaking up in by communicating openly – and just like that my voice came back and I recovered.

Another example was with my chronic acne, which was always heavier on my left side, which is the side of our divine feminine, meaning I was unbalanced in my feminine energy (as I'll be explaining in more detail, the divine feminine and masculine relate to types of energies that we all have, not sex or gender as such). This also related to my sex hormones and womb, which once again was a manifestation of the inner work I needed to do relating to my womb space and feminine energy.

Like fear, trauma can be stored in the body, and my experiences from an emotionally and sexually abusive relationship stayed in my womb space and stomach and manifested as a hormone imbalance (in my chronic acne) and bloating. Now while I took physical steps to help balance both of these through taking supplements, I also explored the emotional root of these problems and saw big changes in my health from working with my mind, body and spirit very quickly after years of suffering.

The body doesn't lie. While there won't always be a spiritual or traumatic explanation for our illnesses or ailments, our bodies will always let us know when they need something or if something is out of balance. So during this process of exploring your beliefs and fears don't forget to listen to your body too.

(I also want to add in here that a condition such as a chronic illness, for example, doesn't always mean someone has to do the inner work; sometimes our karmic contracts mean we're born into this world with illnesses that aren't always linked to trauma or emotions trapped in the body and needing to be cleared. So please make sure to use your intuition and discernment with your health, always.)

So now you know exactly what's contributing to your resistance and fears in life. Remember, it's not just you in charge – think of your mind as being like a control room in which you might think you're the captain of the ship when actually you have your higher self in there too, as well as your conscious mind (you now), your subconscious mind (your programming) and your inner child (your psyche) all in there pressing buttons and directing you in life. So, if you've ever reacted abruptly to something and felt triggered and then later on wondered why you reacted so badly, remember that this means your inner child is pressing your buttons and running the show.

⁺⁺ **PRACTICE** ⁺⁺

Journaling prompts
- "What stops me from manifesting my desire currently?"
- "What core emotions or feelings come up as I think about this lack?"
- "When did I first learn this?"
- "Who taught me this?"

Activity
Use the activity earlier on in this chapter (see page 32) to identify where on your body (and in your chakra system) you feel any resistance or discomfort when I say, "Your manifestation is *not* going to happen." Then use the above journaling prompts to help you explore what's underneath that feeling. Also, which chakra are you being called to work with in connection with this resistance?

Action
Take the time to sit with all I've shared in this chapter and move through the rest of this part of the book as and when you feel ready to. It may be worth taking some time to reflect and identify your core beliefs first and then use the following chapters in this section to help you unravel them further. You may also want to explore the chakras more deeply and which one you're feeling called to work with. I have some chakra balancing YouTube meditations on my channel (see page 211) if you'd like to start working with them.

Feeling Stuck

In life, we can often experience moments or even seasons of feeling stuck, where time seems to slow down or even pass us by. Hours turn into days and days turn into weeks – and before you know it an entire year has passed by and you find yourself thinking, "How am I still in this place?" So many of us experience this feeling yet have no idea what to do to find relief or how to start making changes in our life.

The first step, really, is identifying that you feel stuck. This may be a small feeling or you may feel stuck in a big area of your life. In either case, if abundance isn't flowing and you're sick of your limiting beliefs or fears getting in the way, then the chances are you're stuck right now.

So what causes us to feel stuck in life, I hear you ask.

You see, we humans love routine and we love the familiar. But then we get too comfortable and that's when we find ourselves stagnating, wondering how we got ourselves into this situation. Whether it be with our divine assignments (i.e. our relationships), our career, or feeling caught up in emotions, circumstances, financial reality or even healing, there is a lot that can cause us to stagnate and feel stuck.

A major cause of feeling stuck can come from not listening to our intuition and taking inspired action. If it's in your destiny to leave a certain job, for example, but you've been avoiding taking action and up-levelling, then you may become stuck and stagnate until you make the decision to actively choose the path that's best for you. If you choose the path that's for your highest good and up-level to that new career, this is going to make you really happy, and you'll experience flow and ease.

But if you choose not to take that leap, you will experience yet more stagnation and frustration until you do listen to your intuition and soul.

So we may be actively feeling out of alignment or full of longing, or seeking shift and transformation in the Hurt stage. We may be seeking purpose or a new direction – whatever it is, feeling stuck is a sign that big shifts and transformation are about to happen if we answer the Universe's call and create shift and change in our life.

Sometimes the Universe can even hit us with a life truck, as I call them, where we can have "sliding doors" moments and the Universe has no choice but to step in and help out if we ignore things long enough. You can think of this book as your life truck too – not a sudden and shocking one, luckily, but a reminder and a permission slip for you to take that leap of faith in whatever way you intuitively feel you need to go to honour yourself and your soul. See this as an awakening of sorts: even if you're consciously aware of having a first spiritual awakening, remember that we have multiple awakenings throughout our lifetimes as well as dark nights of the soul, as we go through the healing cycle of death and rebirth in life.

Navigating the Messy Middle

Just like the lotus flower on the front cover of this book, if you are feeling stuck, your situation holds a lot of symbolism. Lotus flowers are regarded in many different cultures, especially in Eastern religions, as being a symbol of purity, enlightenment, compassion, self-regeneration and rebirth. These traits are the perfect analogy for the human experience: even when the lotus flower's roots are in the dirtiest of waters, the lotus produces the most beautiful flower. No mud, no lotus. Without mess we can't be awakened or "enlightened", just as a lotus needs fertile soil to grow. So don't see yourself as being stuck in the mud right now but as being held by the Universe in a sacred container of transformation and believe that your flower and being are going to blossom once again.

Among the chaos you will find the clarity you seek. It's only when we're in the messy middle, as Brené Brown calls it, and on the floor of the arena of life that we start to see the next steps.

Although the energy can feel very stagnant when we are feeling stuck, it can also feel chaotic at times even if there is no movement. The good news is that among the chaos is where we will find clarity, and during the messy middle is where we will discover our next steps.

Being in the middle of the storm is where we find healing. The storm won't last forever but there are important lessons within it that can help you find the light again and enjoy the sunshine. Every season has a purpose, Queen. You have to be in it to win it. When we reframe how we see the messy middle we can understand the layers of possibility, healing and clarity within this space.

Although it doesn't feel like it while you're going through it, think of yourself as being like a caterpillar in the chrysalis, transforming and unravelling the new layers of yourself during this stage. Remember that we are cyclic beings and no storm will last forever, so when the sun shines take a moment to sit and be present – enjoy the warmth and the peace, cocooned in this time of potential. Have gratitude and appreciation for all that is, all that was and all that will be.

The messy middle is a painful place to be sometimes, as we experience a whole manner of emotions and feelings along the ride. The transformation process in the chrysalis during this time can be painful; it can be shadowy, lonely and a scary time – but little does the caterpillar know it's about to complete its transformation into a new lease of life as a beautiful, winged butterfly. This is you right now as we explore the Hurt phase and gather together the information we need to create the container for healing and transformation in Part Two.

Clarity finds us as we let go of what we thought our life should be like or how something would pan out. Only when we step out of our own way can the Universe step in and assist. This is why a great question to ask yourself and journal on when feeling stuck is "What do I need right now?" instead of trying to identify what the problem is. You will find more great prompts at the end of this chapter.

Feeling Stuck and Your Mental Health

We also need to look at this aspect of the Hurt stage from a mental health perspective – I myself experienced depression in my early twenties, which I believe was a spiritual depression. I was stuck in my life at that point and soon as I unstuck myself and found the Law of Attraction and spirituality, my life began to turn around – and quickly. I can also openly admit I've still felt periods of depression over the last few years when I've felt stuck again.

There is a lot of stigmatization around mental health despite there being much more awareness of this subject over the past few years. Sometimes the human mind does need medication to help balance a chemical imbalance, just as it needs love and healing to move through a difficult phase in life. Only you can answer what sort of help you need, but if you have ever experienced depression please don't see this as something that's shameful, wrong or like you're going backward. You're always moving forward – I'm sure there may be times in my future where I could experience feelings like that again – but what's important is having the awareness, loved ones, resources and tools to help yourself spot the signs and take loving action when you need it.

Finding the Energy to Change

Feeling helpless is another indication that you're living outside of joy and are stuck. Although we may feel completely helpless in a situation, there is always something we can do to create a shift. The external world maybe triggering you into feeling stuck or helpless but really this is just a reflection of your inner world.

This played out for me a few years ago while writing my second book, *Positively Wealthy*. At the time I was in my twin flame relationship, which is a really karmic relationship some people find themselves in. Some twins end up together and others don't – there's no set rule and it really does depend on what your soul contract and destiny are with this person. For me, it wasn't meant to last because in the end I chose better, but it took me three years to get there.

Looking back and having done hours of PTSD therapy, counselling, IEMT (Integral Eye Movement Therapy), spiritual modalities and healing since this relationship ended, I can admit I was completely blinded by it. After spiritually awakening in 2016 and learning self-love and self-care, I thought I'd never attract an abusive karmic partner again – but I did. After lots of reflection I can see how toxic and emotionally manipulative the relationship was and how I experienced narcissistic abuse too. I wouldn't have called it that but after seeing a video online about the narcissist abuse cycle it's like they described that relationship perfectly. I was shocked that I had let this happen again but I believe that all twin relationships bring up our deepest shadow work and triggers to help heal them for good. So while I wouldn't wish what I experienced on anyone, the healing and blessings I have now were worth every moment.

The reason why I'm sharing this experience with you is because a lot of you followed this relationship on my social media platforms over the years and probably wondered what happened. I kept going, hoping and wishing that he would change and that this was just all part of the "twin flame journey". So many people online had similar experiences with their twin and, I won't lie, the amount of "just stick it out, they'll evolve eventually and want you again" advice offered by so-called twin flame "experts" was suffocating and one of the reasons why I gave the relationship three years of my life as I felt shame for wanting to leave it.

For two of those years I was stuck in limbo – and keeping myself stuck. I was so sick of waiting, doing the work and not feeling love in my life. I tried everything and I know in my heart I truly gave it every ounce of me, which is when my health started deteriorating. I had chronic stress and dangerously high prolactin (which is a sex hormone made in the pituitary gland) from the stress and uncertainty that relationship continuously gave me – yet I still stayed stuck. It was like I couldn't see that I was the reason why I was stuck and that I deserved so much better.

But it took me time to get to that place and it took me getting so sick and tired of not progressing to finally snap and make a decision that changed my life forever. I had psychics and friends telling me to stick it out because, they said, it would all come good. Every aspect kept me stuck in a toxic cycle and I was miserable, but nothing would change until I did. It was on my 27th birthday in 2020 that I finally decided enough was enough and I couldn't live like this anymore. I went against everything I knew and took the biggest leap into the unknown – with no guarantees whether I'd ever find real and kind love. I risked it all for my happiness, I'd tried everything and felt suffocated and stuck for years, so now it was time to end this cycle.

Soon after this energetic and soul decision, shifts started happening in my life and my healing journey began all over again. Healing came up to the surface week after week and over a five-month period I shed everything from my past and rebirthed myself once again. I kept on clearing things as they came up for quite a while afterwards, but it took around ten months from making that decision to really feel like my true, authentic and happy self again.

In those ten months, my business pivoted several times and I started earning more money than I'd ever earned before by pulling back and not burning myself out. I manifested my beautiful puppy Luna out of nowhere at a time when I had no plans to get a dog until I owned a home with someone. Then, at the same time as Luna coming along, my amazing boyfriend unexpectedly came into my life and the rest is history as they say.

For those two years prior to that, nothing happened in my personal life – it felt stagnant, unhappy and royally stuck. No matter what I tried nothing happened – because I couldn't see that I was the block. I was the one keeping myself small in a negative relationship. It was me who waited on someone who treated me awfully. I was the one convincing myself about a future based on false promises. I was the one who needed to take the action and decide enough was enough. That took strength and that took real courage but thank God I did, because as soon as I said no to something that was not for my highest good and not for me, the things that *were* meant for me said yes so effortlessly. Life began to flow again and become easy; love and happiness were as simple as breathing – and it all made sense.

Get Your Energy Flowing Again

Feeling stuck can come from emotional blockages and from your energetic body (your chakras, for example) not being open and flowing. The key to movement in life is healthy flowing energy, so if you're not moving energy through yourself frequently through various modalities such as dance, walking, yoga, EFT, chakra work, breathwork or even meditation, this can cause energetic stagnation, which can absolutely impact your moods, emotions and abundance.

We very often get stuck on repeat mode in cycles and patterns, whether that's habits and rituals or even negative habits and thought patterns. When your mind is stuck in a loop, you will be emitting the same energy frequency continuously while expecting changes even though your energy hasn't changed. As the famous saying goes, "old ways won't open new doors". Think of energy as being like a radio frequency: currently you're tuned in to one station while your desire or mindset free of resistance is on another station. If you continue as you are, you can't expect to be able to switch stations or frequencies; there has to be an action in order to change the frequency or vibe you're on currently. To change your energy and your reality, you need to break the pattern and loop you find yourself in currently that is causing this feeling of being stuck.

Free Yourself Up

You must act first and then the Universe will follow. That's exactly how this works. So, I would now like you to think about an area of your life in which you feel stuck or helpless and really think about why the situation feels this way – when did this start? Be honest with yourself and reflect upon whether you've tried to create change and shift in your current situation and whether maybe it's time to take a step back. You may not need to exit whatever your situation is, like I did, but you absolutely need to be met halfway and it could be time to step back and step down to allow that movement in. If you're not met halfway then you know it could be an invitation for you to release this now and choose better.

So often our divine assignments – all the relationships in our life, such as our soulmate, karmic relationships or twin flames, and even our platonic and family relationships – are sent to challenge and up-level us in different ways. If we stay stuck for too long by ignoring the signs, ignoring the inner work and ignoring the feelings of unhappiness, this is only going to make things even more intense. At the end of this chapter, you will find a great activity that will help to give you a fresh perspective on what your relationships can tell you about the way you are currently treating yourself and loved ones.

Daily Gratitude Practice

I want to complete this chapter with a practical element to help you navigate both this phase and your journey through the rest of the book. The quickest way to experience small shifts is by creating and maintaining a daily practice. This not only helps you to raise your vibes, but also sets you up for success and a positive day.

It's important to really look after yourself during this time so we're going to create you a fun daily practice that will support you throughout the book, your healing journey and beyond. The key to creating a successful morning routine is to make it manageable and fun. There's nothing worse than someone telling you what to do and it feeling like a chore. This is why the one practice I would strongly advise adding into your morning routine is a gratitude practice. It only needs to take around 10 to 15 minutes, depending on what you want to include. Gratitude can transmute all negative emotions and because of this fact I love suggesting this exercise to my clients.

By expressing gratitude each morning, you raise your vibes, which helps to make you present and in the moment. It also encourages you to feel appreciative of everything you have now – which creates even more good vibes and abundance. Gratitude alone can shift so many things within your life, including your energy.

To create your own gratitude practice, you could simply start each morning by writing down three to five points of gratitude in your journal. An example of this would be: "I am so grateful for my home because it keeps me safe and gives me a peaceful happy space to relax in." It's always important to state your reason why when practising gratitude, as this challenges you to dive deeper and get thinking about why you're grateful for all the blessings in your life.

Once you're done you can read out each point aloud or in your head and say, "Thank you, thank you, thank you, Universe."

When we can appreciate the blessings in our life our whole world expands into an abundance of possibility and positive energy. I would be lost without my daily gratitude practice and I always feel uplifted and ready for the day afterwards.

Once you've done your gratitude practice, you're free to add anything else that feels fun and exciting into your morning routine. A few suggestions could be scripting manifestations (in which you manifest goals by writing about them as though you've already achieved them), journaling, meditation, affirmations, EFT (Emotional Freedom Technique), yoga, stretching, exercise or oracle card pulling. For now, just do what feels good. Later on in the book I will be helping you create a full, in-depth morning practice and I will also be explaining the scientific and financial benefits of sticking to a morning practice!

In the evening, it's also important to end your day in the same way you started it, to clear any negative vibes or stress you've picked up. I would suggest doing another gratitude practice but changing this slightly by just reflecting out loud or in your head on all the moments that made you smile today and then giving thanks for these. I do this when I'm in bed and ready to go to sleep, as it ensures that no matter what happened in the day, any stresses are released before I go to sleep. This means that I go to bed with a relaxed, calm and positive mind and I wake up with this too – creating a positive cycle each day of gratitude and appreciation.

If you like, you can also do some scripting (writing down a few intentions) for the next day, meditation, reading or anything else that will help you relax and wind down for a good night's sleep. I normally advise against doing active practices such as EFT as this moves energy through your body and will mean you have a rush of energy late at night. So make sure you find practices that help you relax – and switch off from your screens right before bed.

Moving forward throughout the rest of the book, I want you to commit to doing your daily practice each day, as this will support you spiritually and emotionally as we dive deeper into the inner work in Part Two: Healing. Normally, when working with clients, First of all I set them up with a solid daily practice so that they're supporting and nurturing themselves during this process. It's important to use handy practices like this to raise your vibes and help move any blocks when you're working on your healing.

✦ **PRACTICE** ✦

Journaling prompts
- "What area of my life do I feel stuck or helpless in?" (Really think about why the situation is feeling stuck – when did this start?)
- "What do I need right now?"

Activity
Our divine assignments can teach us so much and are there to help us evolve and heal, no matter how frustrating it may feel at times. They are our greatest teachers and they are also mirrors of us, so whatever your loved ones are triggering in you currently is absolutely a reflection of the work that needs to be done within yourself.

Make a list now in your journal of things that feel stuck, irritate or anger you about your loved ones; for example, "It annoys me that Paige always puts me down", or, "It angers me that my dad never listens to my wishes."

Next, reflect those statements back on yourself. Write them in the first person and see if they ring true, so, to use our example: "It annoys me that I always put myself down", and "It angers me that I never listen to my wishes."

If you have that aha! moment and can agree that these first-person statements are true, you've hit the bullseye on where some work may need to be done during Part Two of this book. If they don't feel like true statements, then project them out onto other areas of your life. In what other areas do you experience these scenarios? These will give you a clue where you must take action to create shifts.

Action
Create a morning and evening practice for yourself using the suggestions in this chapter (you can always add in more exercises as we go through the rest of the book). Make a commitment to stick to this throughout the rest of this book to help support yourself spiritually and emotionally.

Loss

Loss can look like and feel like many things, but it almost always triggers feelings of pain and hurt. Whether it's the loss of a loved one through death, the loss of a lover, a house, a career, a baby, a pet, a dream, health or anything we hold dear in this life, loss can feel just as intense no matter how big or small it may be. It can also feel confusing and it challenges us to sit with grief, the by-product of loss too.

The reason why I felt loss needed its own chapter is simply because our losses in life lead to our healing by creating the very hurt we wish to heal. I write this chapter with no judgement because every loss is valid and I want to challenge you to read this chapter with no judgement either about your own losses or anyone else's.

Understanding Living Grief

"Living grief" is a term my good friend Hannah used when explaining to me my own feelings of grief. There have been many instances in my life where I've experienced loss, like we all have in small or big ways. But what I didn't realize until this conversation with her is that we can also experience living grief.

While I'd experienced grief from family members passing in my late teens, I felt a deep sadness in my life a few years ago. I'd been sold the dream by so many of having a happy relationship, finding the one, marriage, kids – the lot. As I mentioned in the last chapter, I thought I'd met my dream man but that relationship simply wasn't meant to be and was far from any "dream life".

I hold no judgement of the psychics, or even myself, who felt convinced this was it. I don't because of the way I now understand life works and also the lessons and upgrades it brought me, so that I can be here today healed and happy. But I still felt grief for a life that would never be and a story that would never be told. To which Hannah explained I was experiencing living grief – the loss of a dream and life that once was. She explained how she too had to grieve the loss of her old life when it changed forever within the space of a few months as her chronic illnesses came to the surface and she went from being a healthy, active young adult who could do anything to being bedridden. Hannah had to grieve that healthy and able-bodied version of herself who had an endless world of opportunity and life ahead of her, when her health issues became complex and she needed constant medical attention and care.

We all experience of form of living grief in this lifetime, no matter what it is – it could even be grieving the old version of yourself before a trauma happened.

I felt angry for a long time that I had been "promised" this life and this person, and it was only through my deep reflections and healing that I realized nothing is ever promised to us and the Universe just doesn't work in that linear fashion. When I was watching *The Matrix* recently, a scene in the film described this perfectly. Neo, the lead character, has been dubbed "the one" who could save the rebellion and the Matrix. He goes to the Oracle, who tells people their fate, and asks if he is the one, to which she replies "no" and expresses her condolences. Fast forward to the end of the film, when Neo does become "the one" (sorry for the spoilers!) and asks his guru Morpheus why the Oracle had told him he wasn't, to which Morpheus replies: "There is a difference between knowing the path and walking the path." Meaning that the Oracle didn't tell Neo because he had to learn for himself he was "the one" and walk the path of learning. This fully resonated with me because it's true that if I had known the real path and journey I'd go on with that relationship, would I have given it my all? Would I have learned all I needed to in order to become the version of myself I needed to be? No is the answer.

No, I had to walk my path to learn all I needed to, knowing what I did at the time. If I had realized how deeply triggering and traumatic that relationship would have been, I would have run! That doesn't mean anyone was wrong – it just means it's what I needed to know to learn and heal at the time.

It's Okay to Grieve Your Losses

We are all walking the path that Morpheus describes, but we want sneak peeks and the answers in life as to why we lose something or why it didn't work out. Apply this to whatever situation you feel loss in – and please know your loss is valid and your grief is valid also.

Hearing this brought me so much release and healing. I could also see that so many of us grieve the things that will never be, but often we feel shame or judgement around this as we haven't always physically lost something. Exactly like with a miscarriage, it's the loss of a child who will never be and a life that will never be lived; and for many mothers and parents all they had was a positive pregnancy test or the awareness of their baby, some never even making it to the check-ups and scans. They too must grieve an "invisible" loss and, from seeing my friends go through this, I know they often felt shame for grieving when the world didn't even know what they had lost.

So no matter what your loss looks like, I need you to know it's okay to grieve and it's okay to be angry, to be sad or to feel any emotion that comes up for you. We live in a Universe where everything is temporary but our feelings and memories can last a lifetime. The space where that thing you loved in whatever capacity is sadly no more, creates a loud, aching echo that manifests as hurt.

Now, I don't mean "manifests" in the same way as I do with your positive intentions, but hurt does materialize from your energy and experiences, and if you don't acknowledge it, it can remain with you as a block that prevents you from healing and stepping into your power. Loss is never easy and it can feel like a death (in a metaphorical sense) – a death of that version of you, a death of what once was, although it could even be a physical death that causes this loss too. This sense of death is us purging and shedding that version of ourselves as we adapt to a new way of living and life. The death could feel subtle, like the death of your youth, or it could be a big purge where you feel like you're moving through a phase of death in many areas of your life. This death-like energy can feel dark, haunting and shadowy, but this is all part of our cyclical nature which I'll go into in way more depth in Chapter 7, on Shadow Work.

Loss and Change

What also echoes throughout loss is change, as change starts with a loss in whatever capacity; so is the secret to navigating loss embracing and making peace with change? Whether it be a change in circumstances or an emotional shift, change is the only constant we have in this Universe and lifetime, yet it seems to be the thing that people struggle with the most. I believe this is because change alters us forever as we let go of what we knew and embrace a new uncertain present moment, and of course this can feel scary and uncomfortable.

The one thing we all have in common as humans is we will experience loss and change in many forms throughout our lifetime. Loss and change are the two things we can't stop, hold or fight – just like in nature, they happen as a part of life and we have to ride that wave of uncertainty and hurt, trusting that at some point the stormy seas will become calm and we can enjoy life once again on peaceful waters. Nature is a beautiful reminder of this – in autumn the trees let go of their leaves and trust that, come spring, they will return. They don't cling on, they don't fight because they know the leaves will return again.

At this stage it's important to identify how your loss has contributed to your hurt and what chain reaction has been set off in terms of change and searching within your life. Then we can start looking at how to unravel your loss (and hurt) and work with this to find relief in this stage of the journey. Don't worry – in Part Two, I'll be giving you an abundance of tools and modalities to help transform these feelings and emotions. For now, it's about honouring the truth of what you are feeling.

At the end of this chapter, I will be inviting you to journal upon your feelings around loss and explore what losses have occurred in your life so far and what you feel could have contributed to your hurt. Remember that these can be subtle or big losses in your life – each one is valid. There is also an activity asking you to write a letter to your loss as part of starting the process of acknowledging your grief.

Accepting Loss

When I asked my lovely followers on Instagram what they thought this book was about, a lady replied: "A book on holding on to your vision even when others told you it wasn't true." This really got me thinking, because when I started writing this book back in the summer of 2020, it probably did have that message.

Yet as I sat with this and reflected, I realized that as I and my life had transformed over those 18 months of writing it, my answer to that lady was actually this: I had held on to my vision until I couldn't anymore, and realized that my new sense of self-worth didn't want that life anymore. I held on to my vision and hope for so long against all odds, but in the end it was me who needed to see for myself and realize in my own time that the vision I'd once had wasn't actually meant for me and I hadn't come this far in life and overcome all I had just to feel miserable and unappreciated. Yet I guess also, on the flipside, that lady's statement was still accurate in some respects because I then did hold on to my up-levelled, aligned vision even when others told me it wasn't possible at that stage.

At that turning point in my life, I had so much unconditional love that was starting to find its flow again that it was no longer an option anymore to cling on to what wasn't working, and, against everything I was told, I did choose a new vision. A vision that was there all along – which was to be truly happy in love and with a healthy, happy and aligned partner. I had to grieve many feelings, memories, hopes and dreams along this journey but with each week and month that passed, I began to feel free again and where I was supposed to be.

I share this because in the beginning, on my 27th birthday, I made a bold commitment to myself not knowing how it would all turn out. I risked being on my own and became fully accepting of that. This brought me so much peace, as when I accepted the very fear I had, it could no longer take hold of me. It no longer fed my want to meet someone and instead allowed me to be present, heal, love myself first and be happy.

Looking back, the gift I gave to myself on that birthday was the best decision I could have made. I thank that version of myself every day for being brave enough to say "no more" and walk courageously into the unknown, putting herself on dating apps despite disliking them and going on dates despite not wanting to meet up with lots of people. Because every single time I overcame something – whether it was my fear or rejection because of what I do or believe in, etc. – the Universe didn't disappoint, and every date taught me something about myself and allowed me to feel safe around men again. I had a lot of positive experiences which I'm really grateful for, all leading me to the happiness I have today.

None of this happiness or bliss would have been possible without loss. I notice in my own life, and with clients I've worked with right before they've experienced breakthroughs, shifts, abundance or up-levelled stages of life, that we all experience a loss of some form to make way for this new blessing. You see, if I hadn't shed the old that was suffocating me, holding me back and giving me nothing anymore (it doesn't exactly sound appealing, does it!), I never would have become the version of myself I am now.

Now, loss isn't always about shedding things that are holding you back – and of course losing a loved one doesn't mean that at all. Your loved ones are always around you, even if they aren't here on this plane anymore. Holding you, guiding you, loving you still and wanting you to know they have you every step of the way. But even if you know this, when you lose someone or something, you still have to take a blind leap of faith into the abyss of grief and darkness, not knowing how life will pan out.

Allowing Yourself to Feel the Loss

Once you've written your loss letter at the end of this chapter, I can imagine it'll bring up a lot of feelings that maybe you knew were there or may come as a complete surprise to you. The key here is really allowing yourself to feel every single emotion: allow the tears to flow and let your body release in whatever way you feel called to feel your emotions right now.

You don't need to carry this by yourself anymore because you have this book, you have me and you have an amazing community of Spiritual Queens all here with you too. It's time to take off the heavy weight you've been carrying around on your shoulders and unpack this gently – it's time to find relief and peace once again, Queen. Just because things didn't turn out how you pictured them, it doesn't mean there isn't a beautiful new journey and destination waiting for you. Life can be truly beautiful when we allow, when we flow and when we trust.

Unpacking hurt is part of the three-step process I described to you at the start of this book, which is why it has been carefully curated to guide you lovingly into the Healing phase so that you can proudly shine once again in your healed new version of yourself.

++ PRACTICE ++

Journaling prompts
- "What does loss mean to me?"
- "What is my first memory of loss?"
- "What losses have occurred for me so far in life?"
- "What did I lost within me alongside the physical loss?"
- "What areas of my life am I seeking clarity in currently?"
- "What have I learned from this loss so far?"
- "What can I do to wrap myself up in support and love?"

Activity
I want you to write a letter to your loss. Now, this may seem strange but hear me out. By writing a letter to your emotions and feelings of loss you can start to identify what's underneath this in your subconscious mind and identify where the inner work needs to be done in Part One.

In your letter, talk about how you're feeling currently and really allow any thoughts, feelings or emotions to flow into this letter. Don't otherthink this; allow whatever comes into your mind to flow onto the paper'. An example of a letter could look like this:

Dear Loss,

Right now, the pain feels unbearable and I don't know how I will get through this change or transformation in my life.

Or:

Dear Loss,

I know that deep down you're still there and I know you're that voice in my head telling me I can't manifest love because I've lost you before.

I don't want to direct your letter too much as I really want you to connect to your emotions and pour your heart out into your notebook or journal as you write. Don't overthink this, allow whatever comes into your mind to flow onto the paper.

Once you've finished, if you identify any statements, limiting beliefs or key information that has come up from this exercise, please note them down in your inner work journal to come back to in Part Two.

I would then recommend burning or destroying this letter in a way that feels good to you. Please be careful and responsible when doing this and put your safety first if burning. (You could also rip up your letter, shred it, flush it or bury it if that would be safer.)

As you're burning or letting go of this letter, I want you to hold a ceremony for your loss and say goodbye to it. Maybe reflect on the happy times with loss, or what it's taught you, but I want you to say this mantra as it's burning or being disposed of:

Dear Loss,

Thank you for all you've given me: the lessons, the blessings and the emotions I feel right now. You have shown me what it means to be human and I appreciate that fully, but now it's time for you to fly free and allow me to do the same. I am ready for healing, for transformation and growth and claim this now. I send you on your healing way and allow us both to feel love, happiness and peace. And so it is ...

Then take a deep breath and exhale to let it all go.

Action

After the above two tasks and as we move forward in this book, I want to invite you to be gentle with yourself and allow yourself time to rest and nurture yourself in a way that feels good. Doing this is a great act of self-love that will also help you to navigate change in the best way you can. So take it slowly, don't rush and give yourself time to really dive into this work intuitively and honour what you and your body need at all times.

Slowing Down

You may wonder why there's a chapter titled "Slowing Down" in this part of the book about Hurt. This chapter had been coming through to me for a while and I knew I had to share these teachings in the book – but when I realized it needed to be called "slowing down", it actually made perfect sense in relation to what I'd experienced and what I want to share with you now.

To begin to identify the inner work we have to slow down and create the space. It's so common for us as humans to become numb in day-to-day life in order to cope, whether this is a conscious suppression of uncomfortable emotions or not.

I know myself that I felt numb up until 2020 and couldn't fully access the inner work that needed to come up for me because I wasn't in a space to receive or deal with what would come up. How that changed for me was when, after years of hormonal acne, I went private with my healthcare and finally got diagnosed with high prolactin levels. As I mentioned in an earlier chapter, I was told this was due to chronic stress and that the level was alarmingly high. Thank God nothing more sinister had occurred because of this, and I always thank my lucky stars it was only acne I had after all my poor body has gone through.

I hit burnout shortly afterwards and had to stop everything. I couldn't work, I didn't feel inspired anymore and I realized I'd been working crazy hours, which was not healthy. Over time, I came to understand I had chronic stress and burnout from all the stress from my previous relationship and I was shocked. How could I have let myself get in this place again and why did I do this to myself?

It took my body finally burning out for me to realize I was numb and a workaholic. My lifestyle was not only ruining my hormones, it was also ruining my happiness. So when I started slowing down, that's when the real transformational inner work came up – when I learned divine balance, which I'll share later on in this book, and how to heal my body. Today, I'm a totally different person – I have better boundaries, I've healed and released a ton of deep inner work; I have balance and, at the time of writing this, at least two more incredible manifestations in my life that I've wanted for a while which felt so stuck before.

Why Do We Experience Burnout?

Burnout can show up in many ways. It could be that you feel exhausted constantly; it could be that you lack motivation, inspiration or creativity. Maybe you feel numb to work and life or even numb to your emotions. Many people try to push past this and force productivity, which never works – the Universe will stop you in your tracks each and every time.

I noticed that after COVID-19 first unfolded back in 2020 many people experienced burnout and were forced to slow down. Why did this happen? Well, first of all let's look at some official stats on this.

In February 2021, Sarah Moss, writing in the *Guardian* newspaper, reported that: "An increasing number of people report feeling worn out and unable to cope due to period of sustained stress", alongside the shocking statistic that "60% of people in the UK are saying they are finding it harder to stay positive daily compared with before the pandemic (Ipsos Mori)". In the same article, Steven Taylor, a professor and clinical psychologist at the University of British Columbia, commented that pandemic-related burnout might make people feel "increasingly emotionally exhausted, despairing and irritable as the pandemic drags out". He compared this to what the World Health Organization has called "pandemic fatigue".

Researching these sorts of stats helped me to make sense of what was happening to myself, my peers, clients and followers. Pandemic fatigue sounded so familiar: as we came out of lockdown, I felt tired, exhausted and with a lack of motivation in work; but at the time I was also going through my deepest healing yet. I was relieved that data had been collected to open a conversation about this topic but it also sparked my inquiry more onto a bigger scale of why this was happening to us collectively.

I think that as a collective we all experienced trauma from having our world and our freedoms stripped away from us. Being under constant adrenal stress puts pressure on our whole nervous system, and with the continuous threat to our health, finances, safety, social life, freedoms, travel, family and loved ones and mental health, it's no surprise we were all feeling this.

Not only were we facing a worldwide pandemic but the "Great Awakening" started happening, where many important issues started coming into the light to be addressed in the world. Everyone I spoke to needed to slow down, rest and heal the burnout they were experiencing from pushing themselves for years. If you worked through the pandemic, which most of us did, even from home, you then experienced burnout in another form as you then blurred the boundaries of your home life and your work life. This has left many of us feeling numb, not knowing what direction to go in, and lacking in passion and creativity – which is of course is to be expected when the whole world goes through a big shift like this.

My friend and I were experiencing burnout at the same time and anything that didn't align to our new balanced way of living wouldn't happen. We'd try to force new projects or plans to please our Virgo productive nature, but every single time if they weren't aligned to our new lives, the Universe would stop us and remind us to stop pushing.

When you're lacking motivation and productivity there is always a reason for this – whether it be alignment or timing or both, the Universe is only ever slowing us down to be able to highlight the very things that need our attention, and inviting us to create the space to heal.

Slow Down to Create the Space to Heal

Just like with manifesting, we have to create the space to heal too. Before burning out, I had no time to look at my inner work or sit with anything. So my body made sure I did have the time. This is the sad reality of many people out there who hit burn out time and time again or whose hormones or health suffer deeply because of the hustle culture that exists in our society today.

When we allow ourselves to slow down we lean into the beautiful divine feminine energy, which creates the container for the inner work to come up. Slowing down, going inward and healing are all traits of the divine feminine energy, although personally I've always sat more in my divine masculine energy and struggled to embrace these traits and the feminine energy.

We are cyclic beings surrounded by cycles and seasons in the outer world, yet we actually experience these cycles and seasons within ourselves too. The yang feminine energy is very much the shadow energy, the winter and inner world. So as you slow down and create the space for yourself to pause and listen you are tuning in to your sacred feminine energy. I'll be going into divine feminine and masculine energy in depth later on in the book – but essentially, divine feminine energy exists within us all. It's the winter inner energy that allows us to slow down and go within, receive, heal and feel, and which houses our shadow self.

We can't force the inner work to come up – it's definitely an intuitive process – but whatever needs to come up will always do so at the right time. It's only when we slow down, breathe, come back into our body and become deeply present that we can then witness our shadow and do the inner work.

Our shadow is nothing to be feared; it's simply just a part of us and our polarity nature. "To be a lightworker we must first be a shadow worker", as my good friend George Lizos always says. It's very true. So many of us strive for the love and light when we see gurus, teachers or even influencers online with this energy, but the truth is the only way those people have this light, bright energy is from facing their shadow and finding peace.

Sit in the Stillness

So how do we go from burnout, stress, numbness or a lack of pleasure in life to being joyful and abundant? Well, joy comes from numbness. Work with me here – when I finally slowed down and sat in the silence, sat with myself and my numbness, I was able to feel my body again, feel myself present and witness the inner work that needed to be done. It was finally safe for it to come up to the surface. From there, I was able to release any resistance I had within me that was stopping me from embodying abundance, joy and fun in the present moment.

So the first step is to allow – allow whatever needs to come up in its own divine time. Feel into the numbness and see what is underneath it. What stops you from being present? Why does it rob you of the present moment and disconnect you from your body?

Sitting in the nothingness can be hard – especially when the very thing you want is productivity and results, right? There is no timeline for any of this, but the more still and observant you become, the more you create the space and a container for miracles, your next steps and healing to emerge. It's only when we surrender to the numbness and present moment that the Universe can step in and assist us. We have to give up, let go of our grip and have flexibility.

The perfectionist, workaholic and productivity culture is what stops us from being flexible and flowing with joy and abundance. It makes us rigid, inflexible and almost like a machine, which is scary. Perfectionism also links to the inner child deeply, which we'll be covering later on in Part Two. When we strive for perfection, we are playing into old childhood wounds to feel "enough". So, it's important throughout this process of unravelling and slowing down that you give yourself permission to mess up and make mistakes. We are messy, imperfect humans and in order to heal burnout and stress or do any inner work we must witness and acknowledge that we will get it wrong sometimes and let people down – and neither will make us any less worthy of love or success.

When it comes to healing, we can't control this new direction as we level up and evolve; we have to take that leap of faith into the unknown and know that with our deep surrender and flexibility the Universe can move mountains – and quickly.

Start to Let Go

Ask yourself now, "Can I let go of everything? Can I let this moment hold me?" Now take a moment to reflect on your answers. How does that make you feel when sitting with those responses? What sensations come up in your body?

We as a society have a deep resistance to being held and letting go. So this divine feminine work is very important – especially when we're trying to identify the inner work and what needs to come up for healing. The only way it will is with this surrender and by creating the space.

Imagine a messy room full of clutter: you wouldn't be able to find anything or take good care of the items hidden in the mess. Think of healing in the same way: precious lessons are coming up and the Universe wants to make sure you have the space, time and energy to look after yourself and nurture these divine lessons.

When we flow like water we can be reshaped – which sounds funny, but in order to heal and be the best version of ourselves, we have to allow ourselves to be reshaped and remapped along our journey toward a new destination we have never been able to see before. The real test here is whether you trust yourself, the Universe and your guides to hold you. It means remembering duality and that the light can't exist without the darkness and vice versa. It's now time to let the light in to balance and embrace both energies.

How can you embrace your shadow more without shame or judgement? How can you let everything be what it needs to be right now? How can you take back your power and dedicate yourself to this healing journey right now?

Healing is essentially about balancing, as we will be exploring in more depth in Part Three. It's about the balancing of energies in whatever ways resonate with you and how you're feeling. For me, it has been about balancing self-worth and healing the wounds that stopped me from knowing my worth, alongside looking at what made me work crazy hours and adjusting my work–life balance to create the life I truly wanted. We must look at all three healing pillars of working spiritually, cognitively and practically to embody divine balance and the healing we seek.

So start off today by inviting yourself to slow down, to become truly present and intentional in all you do. Leaning into slowing down can feel hard when you've been so used to adrenal stress for many years or the productivity culture we're sold. Our poor bodies are so used to being switched on and overworking that we must remember to support them too when we slow down. People often become ill when they slow down because their adrenals and nervous system finally have chance to breathe and relax – meaning the body begins to release anything that isn't serving them.

As you know, over this journey we're looking at all three healing pillars so I want to invite you to look at your nutrition too. How can your support and look after your physical body when doing this work? I'm not a nutritionist by any means, so please do seek professional advice on this, but even something as simple as taking a few supplements to boost your immune system and energy (like Vitamin D, Vitamin C and a Vitamin B complex) can make the world of difference to your body when healing and give you natural energy too!

When we slow down, we connect to our body, our breath and our intuition. We can listen deeply and surrender to our healing path unfolding with the help and support of the Universe.

Queen, if you've been running on autopilot for a while now and are feeling that numbness, this is your invitation to reclaim your power, your health and your peace. After all, if you're always racing ahead and chasing the finish line, what happens to this precious moment that you're in?

⁺⁺ **PRACTICE** ⁺⁺

Journaling prompts
- "Can I let go of everything?"
- "Can I let this moment hold me?"
- "What sensations come up in my body when I think about slowing down?"
- "How can I take back my power and dedicate myself to this healing journey right now?"

Activity
Use the permission slip below to give yourself permission to slow down and witness your emotions. Print out this permission slip (also available on my website, see page 211 for the link) or copy it out from the book and place it somewhere where you'll see it often.

Action
With your answers from the questions in this chapter and journaling prompts above, think about how you can lean into slowing down more. Can you schedule time each week to have healthier work–life boundaries? Create yourself a schedule where you can dedicate time to yourself and slowing down.

Permission slip

I (name)... give myself full permission to embrace my feelings, emotions and actively take inspired action to slow down. I allow my body and mind to slow down and create the space for the Universe to lovingly show me the inner work that needs to be done and what stops me from my manifesting my desires. From today I commit to honouring my self, body and emotions and create the space in my life to feel balance and peace.

Signed ....   Date ....

Hurt Check-in

Once you've completed the tasks and actions in Part One, journal on the questions below either here or in a notebook of your choice.

What are your biggest takeaways from this section?

_____

_____

_____

What three things are you going to implement from this section?

_____

_____

_____

What have you discovered within yourself through reading and working with Part One: Hurt?

_____

_____

How has "hurt" been playing out in your life so far?

_____

_____

_____

What do you think contributed to this?

_____

_____

_____

What statements about limiting beliefs and fears keep coming up for you?

_____

_____

_____

What is the core emotion underneath these statements?

_____

_____

_____

What action can you take to honour yourself and your intuition moving forward?

_____

_____

_____

Rating Scale

In the table below, circle your score from 1 to 10 for each quality (with 1 being extremely unhappy and 10 being very happy).

Happiness:	1	2	3	4	5	6	7	8	9	10
Self-love:	1	2	3	4	5	6	7	8	9	10
Fulfilment:	1	2	3	4	5	6	7	8	9	10
Self-worth:	1	2	3	4	5	6	7	8	9	10
Confidence:	1	2	3	4	5	6	7	8	9	10
Gratefulness:	1	2	3	4	5	6	7	8	9	10

Total   =   /60

PART TWO:
Healing

"Sit with it. Even though you want to run. Even though it's heavy and difficult. Even though you're not quite sure of the way through. Healing happens by feeling."

Rebecca Ray

Having identified the exact things causing you pain and blocking your desires, you will be diving into deep emotional healing in Part Two. I will guide you through your own powerful self-healing journey with the tools and modalities that have transformed my life and allowed me to heal old limiting beliefs, fears, trauma and blocks.

By the end of Part Two, you will have reprogrammed your subconscious mind with new positive beliefs, released blocks and be seeing big shifts in your life and in the way you feel already. You will begin to feel more confident and connected to yourself, free from your past and any negative thoughts, and ready to call in your big desires.

Control and Acceptance

As soon as you let go, the path reveals itself. Letting go is more than just detaching, it's also being able to surrender into acceptance with what is and finding peace with all possibilities.

The problem is that as humans we love to control things! Feeling in control of ourselves and life gives us the sense of structure and stability that we all crave. But when walking this spiritual path, very often we are challenged by the Universe to surrender control and to trust in the Universe's plan for our life instead. As an ex-controller myself this was and continues to be a leaning-in process for me where I have to remind myself of this fact. Yes, we do create our lives but how that pans out and fits into the collective plan as well is all in the Universe's hands.

This is such an interesting conversation to have as a lot of people have different views on this topic. Most people who have done the work on perfectionism, control and balancing divine masculine energy with the feminine will resonate with what I said above. For those of you who are where I was five years ago, trying to desperately control everything around you to feel safe, this will be triggering and a "What the heck, Emma, you said we create our realities?!" moment.

Yes, we do, Queen, but remember that the Law of Attraction is only *one* aspect to spirituality and how the Universe works. The reason why we resist letting go and surrendering so much is because we as humans are designed to be attached to things.

We have been wired to strive for control – and our ego/inner child/inner critic craves control too.

The cold hard truth is the *only* thing you are in control of in this world is yourself and your responses and emotions. Everything else is subject to free will and is in the Universe's hands so to speak. So, while we do absolutely create our realities by using the Law of Attraction, one of the key steps in this process is to detach from the need to control the outcomes. When we are lusting and wanting after our desire, we are sending signals to the Universe that we aren't ready yet. Which is what I want to lead on to for all of you who are reading this and longing for your manifestation to happen right now. I want you to sit with this question and answer honestly:

If my desire was to manifest today, am I truly ready for it?

I guarantee your answer is no; mine was too, Queen! If you were *truly* wholeheartedly ready for your desire to come in, you wouldn't be sat here reading this chapter because your desire would already be here!

Divine timing is an important factor that comes into why our desires may not be here yet. But really all that divine timing is, is vibration. If you were truly ready to receive your desire it would be here. So see divine timing as a reminder that the Universe is protecting you. It knows the perfect way to bring your desire to you – and it's simply a case of aligning to that version of yourself. You don't want it to arrive before you're truly ready and not be able to sustain or enjoy it.

If you answered no to the question about whether you're truly ready for the desire coming today, don't see this as a negative. It's just simply a reminder that something is standing in between you and your desire, which is a positive because now you know and can clear it!

The Universe makes no mistakes and it's essential to trust in the timing of your life. This is easier said than done and I know a lot of you will be asking, "But *how* do I let go and find peace with this?!" Well, I've got your back in a later chapter with this, but for now I want to focus specifically on the need to control and how we can find acceptance.

What Causes Us to Control?

When it comes to manifesting, control and acceptance go hand-in-hand, because we can't find acceptance if we are trying to control our life or desire. Really, we need to dig beneath the surface to find out what is causing us to control and even manipulate. Now, I'm not using the word manipulate in a negative way; I myself have done this too along my journey. We can be doing this even without realizing it; remember that the subconscious can be sneaky. It's time to shine the light on that behaviour and be honest. Honesty allows us the space and capacity to witness acceptance over what is currently present.

I've seen a lot of controlling behaviours with followers and clients and I can definitely testify that I've done this too. I can now link it back to my childhood and see how the wound of loss triggered this need to control and feel in control of my life. It has taken me years to unpack this, mainly by learning how to balance the divine masculine energy within me. Inner child work can absolutely help with the need to control too, which I'll be covering fully in a few chapters' time.

The main way to tell if you're controlling your life or desire is if you're trying to prove yourself to someone or something. If someone was to doubt your desire, for example, you would probably be defensive and reactive. We all know that when we are certain and at peace with what is, we don't feel the need to prove anything at all.

Do you feel triggered when someone questions your desire? Do you feel reactive, angry or freak out when you don't feel in control? What about when you feel unsafe – do you feel rageful or even start self-sabotaging? Any of these actions can be a clear sign that you're controlling.

Hey, you may have even been holding the Universe to ransom. No judgement here: it's important we witness our messy selves and hold ourselves in compassion and love at all times throughout the Healing stage.

Controlling can also look more subtle too. I've seen people try to control things like their diet, money, cleaning (the home), organizing and work load (by being a workaholic), etc. We all, to some degree, *love* throwing ourselves into anything that feels safe and certain to avoid the very thing we know we can't control.

So, sit with yourself honestly and think about an area of your life you're controlling right now. What is this covering up? Where do you feel a lack of control in your life? Use your answers to the journal prompts on page 76, at the end of this chapter, to work with the wounds and triggers you uncovered in Chapter 1 and the healing tools in this part of the book.

There's the starting point, Queen – dig into why you're controlling various areas of your life and you'll find the golden ticket to what needs to be healed.

How Do We Stop Being Controlling?

I know many people will want a guide to releasing the need to control but while this chapter will give you many great tools and tips, there is no step-by-step process. We crave a process because – guess what – that's about control too!

Instead, we need to look at the bigger picture here and why you think you needed your desire by yesterday. Yes, please do keep believing in miracles and manifestation because they can and *do* happen every single day – but they happen from a place of surrender and trust, not control and lack. So if you're in search of a miracle, remember that sometimes a miracle can be as small as a shift in perception and awareness.

The truth is that our need for something right now comes from an unhealed place within us – an impatient inner child to be specific. This could stem from anything in our past, so please use the next chapter, on the inner child, to identify what this is and help you release the need for control.

At the end of this chapter, you'll find some great questions and I invite you to journal upon these too to help you identify why you're placing this control on your desires.

Healing Through Acceptance of What Is

We can begin to release our need to control by leaning in to true acceptance, which comes when we can witness what is and find peace with this. This is your next step in the process of healing your need to control.

Many people may resist the idea of acceptance because they have been taught by old-school Law of Attraction teachings that acceptance means you're saying to the Universe, "Hey, I'm okay with this – give me more of it." No, that only happens when you aren't implementing boundaries and you're tolerating what you don't want.

When you find true acceptance and peace, you are no longer resisting or fighting with the ego/inner child/inner critic, which means the Universe can step in and deliver what it needs to because you have awareness of where you are currently and where you'd like to be, however that may look.

Acceptance too can look like many things and I have a few examples of this myself, like when I found myself in £7,000 worth of debt thanks to a not-so-nice ex-boyfriend, which I was left to clear. After finding success with my first business (Extreme Couponing and Deals UK), everything else I was manifesting happened quickly and with ease – yet for some reason the money to clear this debt still wasn't coming!

After six months I had a sit-down with myself as money really was flowing to me – so why was this amount not coming? Well, simply because I had no idea how much being "debt free" meant. I had no awareness or acceptance about the situation; I was avoiding looking at the debt collector's website and wanted to steer clear of the subject all together.

So how could the Universe help me out if I had no clue myself? I was resisting the very thing I knew I needed to have if I wanted to manifest being "debt free" – and that was clarity and awareness. When I sat down and worked out the exact amount I needed to be debt free it was around £6,500, which was higher than I'd thought it would be – but I was still relieved I had addressed and accepted the situation. Within five days of me doing this, nearly £11,000 came to me through a new business opportunity that I'd had no awareness of before! See, the Universe gets to work quickly when we get out of our own way and find peace and acceptance with what is.

Debt can be a big one to make peace with, but, really, I've struggled with doing this to some degree in all areas of my life. My next example is with relationships. I knew exactly what I didn't ever want to experience again after breaking up with my twin flame. I didn't want it so much that I created a whole heap of resistance around it without even realizing.

So, when I started dating again and met a nice guy in 2020, COVID came in and pretty much blocked us all from dating due to the lockdowns, restrictions and the uncertainty it brought. After a handful of good dates between all the interruptions, he and I decided to stay friends. At that stage, I had to truly surrender to the possibility that maybe something more could have happened with this guy – or maybe nothing at all! I really struggled to find peace with this and as he was a karmic relationship he brought up a heap of the inner work I still needed to address – and thank God he did because I did not want to be taking that baggage into a new relationship!

It was only after a few months of inner work and still not feeling at peace and ease that I knew I had to truly let go and accept all possibilities. I was actually pretty good at accepting there could be someone new out there who I hadn't even met yet. So why was I still not at peace? During a healing session using The Emotion Code® created by Dr Bradley Nelson, I had an epiphany as we were clearing one of the many heart walls I had at this time. I now understood that I wasn't feeling at peace because I had built up so much resistance and intolerance to my ex. I was forcing and controlling the situation out of fear, so much so that I realized – how could I be at peace with *all* possibilities when he was still a possibility?'

Now, I knew there really was nothing more to come with him but the resistance I was putting out there wasn't allowing me to be at peace with what is. It was as if I didn't trust the Universe or my own intuition to protect me. I held so much fear that I couldn't possibly be at peace with any other options until I felt at ease with that one. So I worked on removing my resistance and finding acceptance with what is. Yes, nothing else was probably going to happen with my ex, but if it did I could handle it and say no. And the Universe also had my back as it knows what I do want in a relationship. I had been so busy fighting to keep away what I *didn't* want that I was blocking myself from receiving what I did!

I then focused on how I could step back, close the door and feel at peace with the guy I had recently dated too – which was much easier to do when I had made peace with my past and released the resistance and fear I had been holding on to.

I then understood that I could also take action toward opening up to the possibility I could end up with someone completely new – and this felt exciting too. So, I had to meet all three possibilities with ease and an equal measure of peace and acceptance within me. Doing this helped me to then get truly present and find peace and blessings here and now, meaning I naturally let go and surrendered to whatever was to come.

The Universe knew what I wanted in a partner so I didn't need to become desperate or think my options were limited, because, remember, there is no limit on how many miracles the Universe can deliver to us. All I needed to do was release my resistance and relax into whatever was for my highest good.

Finding peace with all possibilities is certainly a hard one to master – especially when you have your heart set on something. I have wanted to manifest numerous things over the years and some didn't happen but other possibilities did.

At the time, it felt upsetting or that I didn't get what I wanted. But trust me, I could soon see that with all rejections in life a divine redirection had happened and I had dodged a bullet, so to speak. The Universe doesn't make mistakes and each and every time I received whatever was for my highest good. I've never been disappointed!

So, I want to do a journaling exercise with you below that I call "Plan B" to help you find peace and acceptance with all possibilities in your life. Because the truth is we aren't in control of the hows, whens, whos or whats – the Universe is, and as I've spoken about above in my own examples, when we get out of our own way, the space for miracles is created.

Ease and grace can flow when we are in the vibration of peace and acceptance over what is; and our desires become magnetized to us when we are in a state of allowing. So follow the exercises below to give yourself the gift of acceptance and to heal and release the need to control – it's not serving you, Queen.

$^{+}$$^{+}$ **PRACTICE** $^{+}$$^{+}$

Journaling prompts
- "If my desire was to manifest today, am I truly ready for it?"
- "What am I trying to hide in my life?"
- "What is this covering up?"
- "Where do I feel a lack of control in my life?"
- "What desire do I want by yesterday?"
- "Why do I not feel ready to receive this?"
- "What is standing in my way?"
- "What's the worst thing that could happen in this situation if I was to let go?"
- "What's my Plan B?"
- "Am I okay with all the potential outcomes and do I trust that the Universe is protecting me here?"

Activity
Work on balancing your root chakra (the chakra for stability and structure) with either the mantras below or meditations online:

- I am stable and grounded.
- I trust in the process of life.
- I am protected and nurtured.
- I am financially secure.

You may also want to tune in and focus on your other chakras if you have identified the urge to control in issues that relate to any of them too.

You could also do some EFT with Brad Yates on YouTube to work through tendencies to control and finding acceptance with what is. Just search for videos on his channel that focus on this topic.

Action
With your answers from the questions in this chapter and journaling prompts above, think about how you can lean in to acceptance more. How can you release resistance and find peace with this? What action do you need to take to meet all outcomes equally with peace, neutrality and ease?

Connecting with Your Inner Child

I first came across inner child work in 2018, the year my real inner journey to face my shadow work and heal the trauma within me began. Since doing my own inner child work I decided to become an inner child healing practitioner and bring these healing practices into my client sessions.

Over the last four years that I've been doing so, I've come to see the inner child as not only the younger version of ourselves, but also the ego (and inner critic). You may resonate with this too as we dive into this work more, but everyone will be different. If it's easier for you to see the inner critic or ego and inner child as being separate then absolutely go with that. But, for me, it's been really useful to identify it this way so that when fearful thoughts or negative inner chat comes up, I can spot when my inner child needs some love and attention.

In popular psychology and analytical psychology, inner child work refers to the individual's childlike aspect or psyche. It includes what you've learned as a child before puberty, but I do believe our inner child can also hold on to events, feelings and beliefs from our teenage years and later.

The inner child can affect many areas of life including how we respond or take action when we are adults. If you feel like your ego (or inner critic) is running the show then you can guarantee the inner child is the real party beneath this. I definitely feel that inner child work is a tool for life, not just to heal one area of your life or trauma.

I approach inner child work through practical, cognitive and spiritual practices because – as you'll know from the themes within this book – this is how you integrate and embody the healing work fully. From my own inner child healing and working with clients, I've also found this method to be the most efficient and effective in seeing big shifts quickly with myself and others.

How to Meet Your Inner Child

There are many ways to connect and work with your inner child, for example intuitively through meditation or by tuning in to your heart centre. Although the inner child will usually appear to you to be a particular age (so let this come to you naturally when connecting and don't force an age on them), they could be feeling triggers or wounds from an earlier or older stage of your life. Inner child work is a very personal practice and relationship, so always go with what feels right for you and what feels true.

In my inner child healing practice that I've cultivated and use on myself and clients, I work with three stages: meeting, healing and embodying. It's extremely important to feel comfortable and confident with each stage before moving on to the next and all three together give the best results.

In this chapter, I will walk you through the meeting stage of inner child work (through a meditation and connecting practice at the end of this chapter) and how you can connect with this beautiful part of yourself and invite more fun into your life. The book as a whole will then guide you through the "healing" stage of inner child work but I do have a specific formula for this available in my "Inner Child Joy" course (see page 211) and in my one-to-one coaching sessions. I would also suggest working with someone like myself or NLP coaches and therapists who specialize in inner child work to uncover this work in a safe space if you start to feel triggered or have trauma to work through.

So, let's get started with the meeting part of the inner child work and why this is so important. Just like with any relationship it takes time and effort to build a loving stable relationship and the same goes with your inner child. There are many meditations online you can do, but many of these simply throw you and your inner child into the inner work without any connection building or tracing the wound or fear back. The inner child won't cooperate if the first stage of meeting hasn't been done or if they feel you're not truly there for them or present.

Inner child work can be very unpredictable as some people can create a connection straight away while for others it can take a good two to three weeks of consistency to hear a reply or feel their inner child is there. If this is your experience please don't worry – I've worked with hundreds of clients on this now and you're certainly not alone! Be patient, loving and allow the inner child journey to unfold as it's meant to.

Top Tips for Connecting with your Inner Child

- **Use photos**: get some photos of yourself as a child and place them on your spiritual altar or where you'll see them regularly over the next few weeks. Look and connect with the photos often and feel that version of yourself within your heart centre.
- **Meditate**: you can purchase the *Hurt, Healing, Healed* meditation playlist from my website (see page 211). On there, you'll find my official inner child meeting meditation, which I use within my inner child course. Listen to this as little or as often as you'd like to over the next few weeks, as this guided meditation will help you to connect with your inner child and build a loving, nurturing relationship with one another.
- **Reconnect**: following on from this chapter's breathing and connecting exercise at the end of the chapter, watch or listen to your favourite films or music from your childhood. Have a dance party or movie night and make it as fun as possible. Maybe you could even eat or drink your favourite food/drink from when you were a child to once again help you to connect to that childlike essence.

Get Ready to Play

Another point to note when first meeting your inner child in meditation is there may not be an end goal. I know many clients whose inner child only wants to play, and who won't willingly go into any past experiences or reveal much until the client does play with them. This is very common for any of you who work hard and have no fun or "playtime" as this is exactly what your inner child is crying out for! So allow yourself to play with your inner child and invite this fun into your adult waking life too to help build this connection.

While you can do all of the meditations, embodying the healing and taking action in the physical realm is just as important if you also wish to see the results in your outer experiences. And even outside of meditation, there are many great ways to work with your inner child and embrace fun, childlike play in your adult life. Ask yourself: how can I have more fun? What would my inner child love to do today to have fun?

For me, sometimes that means playing with my godchildren to spark that fun playtime, or it's about watching my favourite movies I loved as child and growing up. Or even having my favourite childhood meals, which my parents wouldn't let me have often. All of these are great ways to create more fun in your life and help to balance the inner child so you can go into meditation more easily and do "the work" with them.

So, allow yourself to have fun and playtime in your life, because life in general and doing "the work" doesn't have to be serious or feel like *work*. The inner child loves it when you can have fun with your healing, so be more childlike and spend time nurturing yourself.

Elementals such as unicorns and even water creatures such as dolphins are closely linked with the inner child so you could even find ways you can connect to these animals or call on their energy to help assist you and hold the space while you're doing the inner work.

Listen to Your Inner Child's Feelings

As I explained earlier, inner child work can be used for a variety of things, whether healing or just day-to-day self-care. As you connect to your inner child more often, you may feel intuitively when they're unhappy or if something's going on. (That's normally how I identify when any inner work needs to be done.) You could even make it a weekly or daily habit to sit in reflection and tune in to how your inner child is feeling that day.

Sometimes my inner child will even feel emotions before these have come up to the surface for my current self to process, and I may think, "Oh, I wonder why my inner child is feeling angry? I don't even feel angry or frustrated today." Then later that day or the following one, feelings of frustration or anger may come up for me too and I'm ready to see where this originates and allow these emotions to pass through me safely by expressing them in an appropriate way.

Even if you just tune in and have an internal conversation with your inner child when you sense they're not happy or negative inner chatter comes up in your daily life, this can be really healing in itself. Show your inner child love and ask them what's going on. What are they scared of? Then comfort them and reassure them as you would your own child or a young child you know.

After learning so deeply about inner child work, and of course experiencing my own healing with my inner child, I do believe that all limiting beliefs, fears and traumas stem from our childhood. Even if a challenging event or situation happened in your teenage years, that younger version of yourself will be holding on to it and projecting it out into your adult experiences through fear, limiting beliefs, negative self-talk, self-sabotage, addictions, actions, lack of trust in yourself or others, self-loathing, people-pleasing, workaholism, anger toward your family or parents, codependency, struggling to set boundaries, anxiety or depression, perfectionism and feeling unsafe. These are just a few of the clues that reveal you have an unhappy inner child, but don't worry, Queen, I've got your back and you've got this too!

As mentioned, perfectionism is a key trait of an unhappy inner child and something I've always blamed on my "Virgoness" over the years, yet deep down I know this was also an unhealed part of my inner child. As author Mastin Kipp shares, "Perfectionism is the fear of rejection and abandonment in disguise", and I couldn't agree with this more. When I first read this quote, it hit me hard and I could see why I would hold myself to such high standards and be so hard on myself and others when I didn't meet them.

An unhappy inner child can show up in many ways but hopefully this is all shining light on your own feelings and emotions and you can see how everything is connected.

Working with Your Inner Child Can Help

Working with my inner child has changed my life forever and certainly for the better! I was finally able to heal deep-rooted trauma within myself and my patterns and beliefs. All areas of my life started to improve as if by magic because I was doing the inner work and changing energetically how I was showing up for myself with more love and also how I was showing up to the outside world.

Once I'd embodied my inner child healing and started connecting with her regularly, I noticed that I felt more childlike in my approach to life – which made me feel scared for a moment that I was acting immaturely or not taking life seriously.

Once that initial fear had subsided, I realized that through embodying my inner child I was able to have more fun in life away from work and my adult responsibilities and connect to myself more.

I think sometimes it can feel scary to invite this energy into our life as we feel we need to be mature and responsible adults, which, yes, in some respects we do. This is where a lot of our internal issues can come from – when we focus on being a "serious" adult and life then becomes repetitive and boring. This is when the inner child will be crying out for fun and time away from work most, in order to find the magic and sparkle in life again that many of us experienced as children.

I also noticed the more connected I became to my inner child and deepened my practices, the more I would see inner child work show up time and time again in my coaching sessions. Over the 2020 pandemic so much inner work came up for myself and everyone collectively, and this was reflected all of a sudden in a large majority of my clients working with their inner child through our sessions and really enjoying the task of connecting and having fun again.

Another common way most therapists work with the inner child is through a technique called "reparenting yourself". I have never put much focus on this in my own work or with clients because we already do this work through self-love and self-care – so make sure to integrate it into your inner child work also.

Loving Your Inner Child

The inner child absorbs so much from our childhood, teenage years and adulthood, and this is why I knew all along that my inner critic wasn't some nasty ego out to get me, but in fact my scared younger self who was petrified of getting hurt again. Today, I'm able to act and respond to life from a healed, aligned place and recover from any layers coming up much more quickly through checking in with my inner child and seeing intuitively what she's feeling and how she's reacting to the situation.

Try this the next time you're craving more fun in your life or if your inner critic is running the show, and I promise you'll unlock healing – which in turn will help you to feel happy, whole and at peace with all parts of your life and self. It's such a beautiful practice and relationship to experience with your inner child.

I want you to start giving your ego (or inner critic) love every time they pipe up. Instead of getting frustrated or bashing your ego, see this as the small version of yourself who just needs love. Say loving things to yourself; for example, if your ego is insisting, "But you are not worthy of having that desire", respond with something loving to reassure your inner child, just like you would with a small child you know or your own child. You could say something like this, for example:

Little [your name], I see you and I hear you. I'm sorry that you're not feeling very worthy today but I'm here to remind you that you are deeply worthy and deserving of your dreams and you don't need to worry because I've got us, I love you and our wishes will come true.

Keep repeating this process for at least 21 days every time the ego or inner critic comes up for you and note down in your journal what shifts happen as a result and how often the ego or inner critic pops up. You'll find by day 21 onward that your inner child will start to trust you more and you won't feel so attacked with doubt and negativity, as you two will be well on your way to having a harmonious, loving relationship.

And remember that inner child healing work is all about having fun too! So make sure during this section of the book you're having fun and taking time off from the inner work to play with your inner child. This includes manifestation: involve your inner child in your manifestation process. An inner child loves creating and being included so get creative together – this could be a joint vision board you make, dancing together to raise your vibes or even doodling and colouring in your manifestations together. Manifesting with your inner child is a powerful practice as joy is the ultimate creator! Not only does it honour both of your needs and wishes but it strengthens your bond too. So ask your inner child today: "What would you like to manifest?"

Working with your inner child will be a lifelong journey but a very rewarding one that helps you to be present, whole and at peace – which will positively pass down to your children if you have them, and help with your parenting and relationship with them too.

Remember, the most important relationship in your life is with yourself so love that little version of yourself unconditionally because you both deserve to come home to one another and be best friends again.

⁺⁺ **PRACTICE** ⁺⁺

Journaling prompts
- "How can I mother or father myself more?"
- "What does my inner child need from me?"
- "What does my inner child wish they received more of when we were younger?" Action your answer if possible.
- "What does fun mean to me?" Challenge yourself with this one and write a list of 25 to 30 points if you can, as this will challenge you and explore what fun really does mean to you. Once you have your list, make an effort to action one of these points a week.

Activity
Place your hand on your heart centre (in the middle of your chest) and take a deep breath in. On the exhale, release and let go of any tensions or stress from your day so far. Close your eyes and focus on your heart centre and, when you are ready, set the intention to bring forward your inner child. You might see them, hear them or sense them. Once you can feel your inner child present, ask them these four questions and listen for their response:

- How are you feeling today?
- What do you need from me right now?
- What do you want me to know right now?
- What do you want to do for fun this week?

Be patient and gentle with this practice as it can take time to hear or sense clear responses. Try the meditation and other tips mentioned within this chapter and keep doing this activity a few times a week to strengthen and grow that connection with your inner child.

Action
For the next two to three weeks work on cultivating a loving and nurturing relationship with your inner child through the top tips in this chapter and with my meditation playlist (see page 211). Dance, manifest and play with your inner child and make sure to action your responses to the activity above, each week.

Shadow Work

I first heard about shadow work about three years into my inner work journey and I won't lie – it scared me. It scared me to look at my shadow, which felt like a dark and heavy energy I preferred not to think about. See, the thing with "toxic positivity" is that it makes us feel like we must be "love and light" all the time, which essentially suppresses our shadow self and ourselves in the process. I personally don't believe in any positivity being toxic because it's not, it's just negativity and low energy. Positivity isn't toxic, it's love; it's just not always being taught in this way.

My shadow self felt heavy, dark, scary and bad to think about. I'd been advised to not dabble in that from mainstream Law of Attraction teachings and to focus on love, light and positivity instead. It's only when a good friend of mine came on my podcast and said, "People think I'm all love and light and angelic, but, Emma, the truth is I'm only able to be this love and light because I've faced and embraced my shadow self." This really struck me as this lady is so pure, full of love and caring – but she owns her shadow self too and isn't afraid to show that. This got me thinking about my own journey and I knew it was time to face my shadow self no matter how scary it felt.

Shadow work can be defined in many ways as you'll see throughout the chapter, but for me, American spiritual teacher Teal Swan hits the nail on the head when she describes our shadow as being nothing more than the part of us that is unconscious and therefore hidden from our awareness. Our unconscious is filled with all kinds of things that we have judged to be "unacceptable" about ourselves, and shadow work is nothing more than the art of making the unconscious, conscious and the unacceptable, acceptable.

Even if this is the first time you've done this, when you tune in to your shadow self, it most probably feels unacceptable, bad, shameful, dark and very often it may feel as if you are unworthy of love as well. I know it was like that for me.

Having worked with hundreds of one-to-one clients over the years, when I bring this work up I often get a mixed response. Some are like, "YASS, let's do this, Emma – I've heard lots about this and I'm ready!" Or, alternatively, I get: 'But isn't it bad Law of Attraction to think about negative things?" and "I don't know how I feel about this – I'm love and light, I don't have a shadow self." No one response is right or wrong here, although it's just interesting how the work can trigger people and that some people will not accept shadow work as an important part of their healing journey. So let me break this down for you, as this chapter covers a few aspects of our shadow self and I want you to understand where I'm coming from with these themes.

Understanding Polarity

We live in a world of polarity, even within every single human – no matter whether we identify as being male, female or non-binary, for example – we all have divine masculine and divine feminine energy within us. The left-hand side of your body is traditionally thought of as your feminine side, while the right-hand side is your masculine.

You may have heard of yin and yang energy before. Together, they form an ancient Chinese symbol of harmony, which reminds us that life is a balancing act and most fulfilling when we learn to embrace its dualities. It's about embracing the ups and downs, the good times and bad and joy and challenges that may arise.

I would like you to visualize the yin-yang symbol as I explain the dualities or polarities in this work to you.

The Divine Feminine and Divine Masculine

Let's begin by looking at what is meant by the divine feminine and divine masculine energies (which I've mentioned briefly before), how these affect us and how we can learn to balance these and find harmony, no matter what gender we are or we identify with. Traditionally, women are said to embody the divine feminine and carry that energy as a collective, yet each individual woman will also have both the divine feminine and masculine within her. The same goes with men, who are traditionally linked to the divine masculine: each man will also carry both energies within him too.

Now, these traditional polarities obviously won't apply to everyone and I want to be clear that they are not fixed – nor do I want to put labels around these energies. The energies could apply very differently to someone going through a very different situation to me, for example, and more than anything, only you will know what resonates and is your truth.

Where this gets a little more complicated is what energy we primarily sit in; for example, even though I am the divine feminine as a woman, I actually sit more naturally in my masculine energy and have done throughout my life. I even discovered in an energy healing session that I chose to embody more masculine energy in this lifetime to learn how to love this and not abuse it like I have done in previous lifetimes. So we will have one energy that we sit in more than the other, whether it's balanced or unbalanced.

I came to realize that I had abused and suppressed my feminine energy for years before doing my shadow work, and I hated things like my period, my body and being gentle. This didn't mean I didn't enjoy expressing myself as a woman during this time and enjoying more feminine things, but, as I said, we all have both energies within us so we will reflect both aspects. I loved thriving in my masculine energy, which also was unbalanced – so, yes, both of these energies can be balanced or unbalanced at different times.

The divine feminine and masculine energy within us can become unbalanced, just like our energetic body and chakra system. They can become unbalanced through societal and childhood conditioning, toxic traits, experiences, trauma – essentially the Hurt phase.

There are a few signs to help you realize when one energy is imbalanced; for me personally, my high prolactin and hormonal imbalances were a reflection of the imbalanced feminine energy with me. This is sadly a common theme for women who sit more in their masculine energy and who work hard (to the extent of abusing their masculine energy). I've known countless CEOs, managers and hard-working women lose their periods or experience hormonal imbalance because they're not listening to, slowing down or embracing their beautiful feminine energy. This will look different for everyone, though, and you may not always have a physical symptom alongside the imbalance.

Below, I've put together some key traits to help you identify whether your feminine and masculine energies are balanced or imbalanced:

Feminine Unbalanced

- Rejects their menstrual cycle, womb space and/or sexuality and pleasure.
- Needy, codependent, overly sensitive.
- Doubts themselves and their decisions.
- People-pleasing, unable to express their own needs and boundaries.
- Compares themselves to others
- Low self-esteem/self-worth.
- Doesn't take action and struggles to launch or complete projects/tasks.
- Puts everyone else's needs above their own.

Feminine Balanced

- Connected to their womb space, periods and/or sexuality and embraces aligned pleasure.
- Knows their self-worth and has healthy loving boundaries in work and personal life.
- Mothers themselves and allows themselves to express/feel their emotions and be gentle/soft.
- Allows themselves to be vulnerable and held.
- Connected to their intuition and inner/outer cycles.
- Embraces their shadow self and does the inner (emotional) work.
- Compassionate and loves unconditionally.
- Sexual and loves their body.
- Creative and can express their creativity and self.
- Able to express anger and passion.

Masculine Unbalanced

- Ruthless and toxic behaviour toward themselves, others and the feminine.
- Selfish and manipulative.
- Forceful and controlling.
- Egotistical and sees themselves as separate.
- Easily threatened, stubborn and headstrong.
- Argumentative, prone to burn out and perfectionism.

Masculine Balanced

- Achieves goals in a balanced and healthy way.
- Strong, protective and supportive.
- Proactive, abundant and the energy of manifestation.
- Powerful, energized, confident and passionate.
- Able to be supported and held by the feminine.
- Loves unconditionally and is empowered.
- In touch with their feelings and connected.

Rebalancing Your Energies

Now that you know what to look out for with any energetic imbalances of the divine feminine and masculine, I hope that you can identify where some work may need to be done. Meeting so many women during my career, I've been saddened to have seen so many feeling such disconnection from their periods, womb, body and pleasure.

Having done this feminine balancing work myself over the last few years, I have found it extremely powerful and healing. It has enhanced my relationship with my body, pleasure and sex – meaning I can enjoy all of them from a balanced space and embrace my beautiful sacred feminine energy too.

At the end of this chapter, I'm going to put some tasks and practices for you to complete to dive into these energies more deeply to help balance them. Please work with the questions that resonate and apply to you; or, if you want to, you can do all of them if that would feel good. Use your intuition to decide where to go first and have fun exploring them!

The Law of Polarity

Essentially, all of the polarities I share in this chapter come under the Law of Polarity. The Law of Polarity is the idea that everything has two "poles" or extremes that balance each other, such as love and hate, good and bad, light and dark, and we need both polarities if we are to live in harmony.

Think about it, if all we ever had were good days, how would we know what a bad day was? And how would we know what defines a good day if we've never experienced the opposite?

The Law of Polarity teaches us gratitude and appreciation for both polarities. Without sadness we'd never experience happiness. This is why we need our shadow self – just like we need happiness and sadness and all of the other pairs of opposites.

Your shadow self represents your hidden self and the version of yourself that you hide away, or the traits that you deem too negative for the world to see. But whether these are guilty pleasures, behaviour or thoughts we don't consider as being socially "acceptable", we all have these within us.

Shadow work refers to uncovering this version of ourselves and becoming accepting and loving toward these traits, behaviours or thoughts. This being said, you may need to do some inner work around why you do certain things or have certain thoughts if you feel these shadow aspects need to be stopped or aren't healthy.

You see, your shadow self is here to stay, just like your inner child. I think of the shadow self as being like our ego, inner critic and inner child – all trying to protect us and keep us safe. That's why we hide aspects of ourselves or deem things unacceptable as we want to feel safe and loved.

This inner work also tackles disconnection. When we feel disconnected from ourselves, it's because we are not fully embracing all aspects of ourselves and the disconnection is a result of that suppression. Well, this book is your permission slip to reconnect back with all these beautiful aspects of yourself and come back into this present moment and your body. Your shadow self is just the version of yourself that needs some love, and that wants to be seen and held.

Our higher self actually needs us to be able to express our messy authentic human side and to embrace our shadow. Our higher self is the version of us that has worked through resistance, limiting beliefs, fears and trauma and is living in true alignment and happiness. It is the highest version of ourselves that we have come here to embody and that version of us guiding us all of the time alongside our spirit team.

So, as you can see – just like the yin and yang, divine feminine and masculine – both aspects of ourselves need one another if we are to live in perfect harmony and balance. Neither is good or bad as such, as both create equilibrium and balance in the Universe – all phases and polarities serve a purpose. The same goes with your shadow and higher self: we need both aspects if we are to create fulfilment, healing and harmony.

Working with the Seasons of Life

In an earlier chapter, I mentioned another polarity in life that is created by the seasons: the feminine (yin) energy represents winter and the masculine (yang) energy represents summer.

The earth's seasons bring new energy into our life each and every year. For example:

- **Spring** brings in change, shift and positive momentum as we return to the light and start to see our hard work pay off.
- **Summer** brings in manifestations, and a time to celebrate the light in your life while ensuring you have balance. It's about calling in your full power to be fully seen.
- **Autumn** brings in change once again as the leaves teach us how beautiful it is to let things go – it's a time to celebrate the harvest and all the abundance you've received in the year so far and to look at your focuses as we start to retreat inward, into the darker months.
- **Winter** energy is all about the deep feminine inner journey and it's a time for reflection, inner work, healing, shadow work, rest and recuperation before we head into the lighter months. It's a time to celebrate the past 12 months and set new intentions for the coming year.

These seasonal changes are marked every three months by the equinoxes and solstices. You can do rituals and ceremonies to celebrate these and call in their themes and energies. I have blog posts on my website that can help you do these rituals, but here are some suggestions for you. (The dates below refer to the Northern hemisphere, but as the winter solstice in the Northern hemisphere corresponds to the summer solstice in the Southern hemisphere, please adapt them for where you live.)

Spring Equinox (Usually 20 or 21 March)

Spring clean your home and create a shift in your energy and environment by having a good declutter physically, emotionally and spiritually. Start taking action toward your goals and begin creating in whatever way you feel called to. To create new energy in your life, try something new.

Summer Solstice (Usually 20 or 21 June)

Celebrate the lighter months by getting out in nature or moving your body in whatever way feels good to you.

Celebrate the light in your life and all the things that are going well for you. Also look at what you need to illuminate as you head into the darker months.

Autumn Equinox (Usually 22 or 23 September)

Write a gratitude and appreciation list for all you've manifested and achieved throughout your year so far. Look at what you need to focus on for the rest of the year to help you achieve your remaining goals. Declutter your home and energy with a good clear out to attract change and new abundance in your life.

Winter Solstice (Usually 21 or 22 December)

Reflect on the year and what worked well and what you'd like to improve in the New Year, and write this down on a piece of paper. Then invite in the light by lighting a candle. You could then burn your reflective list safely with this candle to let the last year go energetically. Slow down and pause – how can you rest more and be gentler with yourself?

As well as the earth's outer seasons and their celebrations, we also have our own inner seasons that shape our energy. Again, please use the descriptions above to help you navigate the meanings of each of these when you find yourself going through them. Your inner seasons are why you may sometimes have periods of more outward-facing masculine energy, where you're manifesting and experiencing new things; while other times you may feel more inward facing, connected to your emotions and focused on the inner work with a wintery feminine energy surrounding you.

Also, women and people with womb spaces will also experience further inner cycles with their menstrual cycle. For me, this next cycle has been a game-changer in terms of how I live my life and my focuses around each stage of my cycle every month. I hope that by sharing it, it can help you exercise, eat and live more intuitively with your cycle too:

- **Inner spring (follicular stage):** This is a time to initiate and begin. You may feel like your energy is coming back at this time and you can start to do your regular exercise and movement.
- **Inner summer (ovulation phase):** This is a time to expand and be bold as your energy returns. It's a time to get out there, fully express yourself and have fun.

- **Inner autumn (luteal phase):** This is a time to connect and complete anything you may need to in work or at home. You may feel your energy come down a bit now as you gently head inward, toward your period.
- **Inner winter (period phase):** In this time, as you bleed, it's a great opportunity to reflect and rest. It's also known that during our bleeding phase we are at our most powerful and intuitive, so use this as a time to tune in and connect to your feminine power.

As you can see, the seasons and energies play a big part in our life and energy. Even though they are polarity energies they balance one another, just like yin and yang do.

The Natural Cycles of Death and Rebirth

The seasons can teach us so much about our own life and experiences. As we go through these inner and outer seasons and cycles, we experience a death and a rebirth. This is true whether we apply this to our menstrual cycle, the leaves on the trees shedding in autumn or even examples in our own lives when something fell away, allowing space for the new.

Throughout my life I have experienced many death and rebirth cycles, and each year since my spiritual awakening I feel I've met a new version of myself and shed an old version. It can feel scary to do this but as I shared earlier in Chapter 3 on loss, the changes that happen to us and the world are part of the natural cycle of death and rebirth.

The shedding of the old and the blossoming of the new can be seen all around us in nature – from the caterpillar transforming into the butterfly and plants withering away in winter to be rebirthed again in the spring. During this work, you will shed layers and versions of yourself as well as meeting and embodying these new versions.

The important thing to remember here is that we will all have these cycles throughout our lives as part of our healing journey. Getting to the Healed space may be your summer, full of the energy of rebirth, but that doesn't necessarily mean you are done. At a later phase you may need to pick this book back up to tackle another situation or experience as you experience that change and death again. How often and how noticeable these seasons are will depend on what you need to learn and your lessons, so embrace each one as it comes and go with the flow.

Get the Support You Need

Going through the death phase of winter energy can feel dark and lonely, and you may even feel bouts of depression or anxiety. I know I am prone to feeling this as I've experienced both in my life and recently I was reminded of this when a hormone imbalance made my inner winter phase even more challenging with feelings of depression. Luckily I picked up on this and turned to my hormone balancing tools (such as seed cycling and supplements) and within a few weeks I felt like a whole new person again!

So please do make sure you support yourself too in these phases in whatever ways you can and please take the right course of action if you're experiencing periods of depression. Also know that you don't have to do all of this by yourself. For example, I have a team of people around me, supporting me in my business and my home life, and I also work with therapists, energy healers and coaches. Sometimes we need that extra support and it is powerful in itself to allow yourself to be held and supported in these times – so please do reach out either to me or someone you resonate with to work with you if it feels good to do this.

Be Kind to Your Shadow Self

For so long people have bashed the inner critic, ego and inner child – all aspects of the shadow self – believing it's some dark version of themselves that should never see the light of day. But, really, as I described earlier, it's impossible to live in an authentic space of high vibes, love and light and positivity without creating harmony and balance with *all* aspects of yourself. You can't be truly aligned and authentic if you are shaming or suppressing aspects of yourself.

Society teaches us that we need to be "the good girl" for example or that we can't be multi-dimensional beings who love fashion, technology and are deeply spiritual. Or a devoted yogi who also loves Lizzo. But why can't we be it all? Why can't we love, honour and express all aspects of ourselves? Because we're taught that we must fit in certain boxes to be approved of and loved. We're taught this in school from a very young age, so now as adults we are afraid of expressing that shadow self of ours for fear it will be seen as too negative, too much, too this or that and we'll be shunned from society.

The real shadow work is witnessing your shadow and all the multifaceted parts of yourself – and still loving yourself unconditionally. It's about holding space for all those versions of yourself, past and present, and witnessing them without judgement and with compassion. It's recognizing that our shadow self is not something that needs to be hidden but in fact holds the very secret to bringing balance and harmony into our life. When we have faced our shadow we have faced our true self and can learn to love and express ourselves in an aligned and authentic way. When we then express our true self, and love and see our shadow, we create the container for healing, abundance and miracles to arrive.

Loving my shadow self allows me to have more compassion for myself and to acknowledge my guilty pleasures and thoughts. These may not always be "spiritual" or "high vibe" but recognizing them creates equilibrium and non-duality over separation.

If we keep disconnecting ourselves through separation and duality, we create a great sense of dissatisfaction with life and ourselves. Again, something that is massively taught in the Law of Attraction sphere is that the shadow self is some sneaky thing that needs to be eliminated. Fortunately, the shadow self is not like a Dementor from *Harry Potter* that needs to be expelled with a simple "Expecto Patronum" spell. The shadow self is here to stay, the shadow self is you, the shadow self is not separate; nor is it here to hinder you.

Your shadow self loves you; it wants to keep you safe and it has been taught to hide itself to protect you. But, Queen, you don't need to do that anymore. On the other side of duality and separation is a beautiful healing where you come back home to yourself and love yourself unconditionally (which we'll work on in Part Three of this book).

Moving forward, it's about focusing on these polarity energies and making sure we are listening to and honouring them while also having the understanding that one is not better than the other and we need to embody both to truly live a life full of confidence, abundance and aligned energy. Alignment creates abundance and the only way you can be in true alignment is by embracing every part of your beautiful self. *That* is how you live a high vibe authentic life and become a true Spiritual Queen.

✦✦ SHADOW WORK PRACTICE ✦✦

Journaling prompts
- "What aspects of myself do I feel are hidden or shameful?"
- "How would I live my life if I felt safe enough to express my true authentic self?"

Activity
Moving forward, follow the suggestions on inner and outer seasons described on pages 90–3 in this chapter and work on balancing your divine feminine and masculine energy with the tips and tools provided below.

Action
From today, commit to holding the space for your shadow self and work toward acceptance. Look at how you can create balance within yourself and love and honour those aspects of yourself you deem unacceptable, wild or needs to be hidden. Think about how you can show your inner child more love and teach them that it's okay to express their true self.

⁺⁺ DIVINE FEMININE ⁺⁺
BALANCING PRACTICE

Journaling prompts
- "What does the word 'soften' mean to me?"
- "How can I soften more?"
- "How can I mother myself more?"
- "How can I slow down and be more compassionate?"
- "What is my relationship around my menstrual cycle/ sexual organs and my body?"
- "What do I think of my menstrual cycle and womb currently?"
- "What can I be grateful for with my sexual organs and/or menstrual cycle?"
- "How can I receive more and allow myself to be held?"
- "Do I feel pleasure in all areas of my life?" If not, how can you invite more pleasure into daily life?

Actions
If you're a woman who has a womb and/or periods, start to work with your inner menstrual seasons and honour this energy. Work to embrace your womb's cycles and harness their power. Learn how to connect and feel into your womb space through meditation, touch and pleasure. Embrace feeling grateful for your period and fertility and learn to love and celebrate these aspects, not shame them.

Also identify if there is any trauma, limiting beliefs or fears within this space or connected to sex or pleasure, and work on these within a safe space or with an expert. Slowly, in a way that feels good to you, de-armour yourself in whatever way that resonates, as to not re-traumatize yourself and to go at your own pace you feel comfortable with.

Connect to your sensuality and pleasure: how can you feel more pleasure with yourself and in everyday life?

Allow yourself to go slower in life and take things at your own pace, honouring your outer and inner seasons.

Mother yourself more and identify what you can give to yourself and your inner child to reflect this.

Allow yourself to be held and supported and embrace receiving in all areas of your life.

✦✦ DIVINE MASCULINE ✦✦
BALANCING PRACTICE

Journaling prompts
- "How can I be more supportive and hold the space for myself and others?"
- "What areas of my life do I not feel confident in?"
- "Where do I need to take more action or make decisions in life?"
- "Do I abuse my power in any way?"
- "How abundant and successful do I feel currently?"
- "Do I feel I control any areas of my life or want perfection?"
- "How can I create more abundance in my life?"
- "What is one thing I want to do but I'm too scared to start or try?"

Actions
If you're a man, reclaim your vulnerability and make sure to be firm and commanding but also supportive and nurturing to yourself, loved ones and the divine feminine around you.

Accept accountability and take consistent action toward your goals.

Work on balancing your force and making sure your drive is coming from a balanced space.

Learn to be present in your inner summer phases and embrace the joy and abundance around you.

Set regular goals and manifestations and take action toward these – seize opportunities and take leaps of faith that feel good to you.

Blame and Forgiveness

A while ago, I came across a post from author Shaman Durek in which he said, "Forgiveness is a mental trap that keeps us stuck in energetic limbo. It's pointless." And I thought, "Woah, but forgiveness is the key to everything!" Then I read on and realized that what Shaman Durek was saying summarized exactly the thoughts and feelings I had on forgiveness and blame too.

Over my three books, you've seen me moving through the three stages of Hurt, Healing and Healed, and I've shared what led me onto my spiritual path and the soul lessons that have occurred for me since. Forgiveness has been a big lesson for me and even now, all these years later, I can see it's a subject that still needs some looking at.

I originally learned along my journey that forgiveness meant understanding why someone did something and then extending forgiveness to this. But what I see time and time again – and I absolutely hold my hands up to this too – is that this kind of approach can become food for the ego. What I mean by this is when people extend forgiveness in this way, it's like they are "blessing" the other person with their acceptance and forgiveness along the lines of "it's okay, I forgive you", when this actually creates division, duality and hierarchy. Of course, it's important to apologize when we feel we need to and it's nice to receive an apology too – but "blessing" someone with your forgiveness only prolongs the healing journey.

This sort of approach to forgiveness invokes the energy of pedestalling (and I know I've felt this myself), when really the true, core energy of peace that we should be striving toward with forgiveness is radical acceptance – which means finding peace with the reality of a situation without necessarily agreeing with it.

This is not to take away from anyone's experiences or traumas – those are all absolutely valid and real. But we also need to look at blame and realize that when we still blame someone deep down, we can't really forgive them and we can't reach peace or acceptance.

Once again, it's also about using our discernment. If someone has hurt or upset you, is this something you want to give them the opportunity to do again? Yet your discernment can still be an act of radical acceptance – for example, if it means walking away or not having that person in your life anymore. It's about finding a middle ground in all of this and the way we look at it too.

Forgiveness, Blame and Our Inner Work

Forgiveness can create a blame and punishment culture. We've all seen this play out when we may say that we have forgiven someone, but we really still hold a grudge and then say, "Well, it's okay for me to do this, because you did that", or, "Well, you did this to me." Whether it's in an argument or maybe something more subtle than that, people can use forgiveness as a way to control others and pedestal themselves even long after the event. All this does is create further separation and duality, which might make us question whether we ever really forgave the other person in the first place.

But it can also trigger the inner work we have to do, meaning we may seem to forgive a person on the surface, but deep down we continue to feel blame, shame and judge ourselves or the other person because of a wound within us that still needs to be healed.

As I look back at my teachings and journey, I realize that I too was looking at forgiveness mistakenly and still creating duality around wrongdoing and rightdoing. It's not about saying what someone did is right or acceptable; it's looking beyond that and saying, "How can I find acceptance?"

Radical acceptance came for me when I accepted what was, what is and what will never be. I've had to move past karmic lessons and emotional and sexual abuse – all of which made me angry and upset that I'd had to experience these things. While they are not okay, I came to a place in my journey where peace could only reside within me once I had reached a place of acceptance rather than forgiveness.

People will hurt one another and do terrible things; believe me, I'm not saying this journey to acceptance is a walk in the park, as it takes dedication and healing. There are also sometimes no answers to the awful things that happen in the world – but the Universe is challenging us to look beyond right- and wrongdoing and meet both ourselves and the other person in the middle by finding radical acceptance.

In the post I mentioned earlier, Shaman Durek goes on to explain: "Acceptance sets us free while allowing us to stay engaged, because when we accept, we are relating in the realms of truth. We are not denying, and we are not blaming, and we are not victimizing, and we are not judging. We are simply acknowledging. This happened. This is an energy or an experience that we shared, and that had an impact on everyone involved, and what they choose to do with those energies and those lessons moving forward is up to them."

Compared to this approach, the style of forgiveness I'd previously learned on my spiritual journey was very much based on the Western self-help ways. I then reflected upon books about Buddhism and realized I actually resonate with the Buddhist teachings of unconditional love and acceptance more than the Western teachings. Why? Because the Western way, I feel, keeps us stuck in a loop and in the Hurt phase – whereas the journey of radical acceptance brings us back home to unconditional love, which of course is the aim of the whole healing journey and the goal of this book.

The Lessons of Post-traumatic Stress Disorder

During the process of writing this book I was diagnosed with PTSD (post-traumatic stress disorder). I was shocked and confused as to why I was having flashbacks and other physical symptoms almost out of nowhere. I was in a calm, happy and loving space where all was well and I had such amazing loving people around me – so it made absolutely no sense why this would come up now. Then, when I started working with my therapist, I began to understand how often things like PTSD come up to the surface when you're in a happier place in your life. My good friend Hannah explained how her PTSD around her health issues also came up when she was feeling more stable and happy – not during the traumatic times.

The reason why this happens is because our bodies go into fight, flight, freeze or fawn mode to survive at the time of a challenging event; and it is very common for some people to stay in survival mode physically and emotionally even afterwards. Once the event has passed and your body's nervous system regulates again (because it feels safe), then the illness or cognitive effects can truly be seen. It's important to realize that at this point I was in the Healed stage and this was simply another layer of my trauma and experiences coming up to the surface to be released and healed.

I could have got mad, I could have got angry that after all I'd been through and the years of therapy and healing that followed my last relationship, I then had PTSD to add to the list. But I didn't – I got still and I got present and realized how far I'd come and how blessed I am to be in a new phase of my life with the most incredible people. I didn't let my PTSD define me or become an identity (we'll cover this more in depth in Part Three). We create identities throughout our lives and my PTSD was creating a survival identity, which meant even though I'd manifested incredible things and am now in such a healthy and loving relationship, there was still an identity within me that wasn't yet fully present or healed, which meant that I was keeping myself stuck with one foot in the present and one foot in the past.

The reason why I'm sharing this with you now is because it would have been so easy to blame my past for the PTSD and the hours and hours of sessions, coaching and healing I've had over the years – but what's the point? That would only hinder my healing further. When I witnessed the memories and trauma that came up in my PTSD sessions with radical acceptance instead of judgement for myself or the other person, I was able to reach the middle point of right- or wrongdoing and realize all these life experiences were shaping me into the healed Queen I wanted to be. These were my soul contracts and my karmic lessons all playing out exactly as they were meant to.

How to Reach Radical Acceptance

Accepting that we are always where we are meant to be can be comforting, but it can also be very hard to do when someone has hurt us. But staying in victim mode only keeps us stuck.

Instead of letting an event or experience become who you are or determine your identity, look at it as a part of your story – it doesn't define you.

When I go on podcasts or do interviews, people are always keen for me to discuss my exes, as they did shape my experiences for nearly a decade of my life. But it got to a point where I was willing to talk about my relationship history only to provide a bit of context and not allow this to become an identity or take over the goodness that I now want to share about life and my work. I wanted to leave it in the past and drop that identity, but how could I when people would want me to relive it every time I was interviewed? Of course, I am extremely grateful for all of those karmic experiences for getting me on my spiritual path, purpose and to a Healed state – and so there is no blame.

I realized that for so long, and even in my first book *Spiritual Queen*, I was still blaming and pedestalling in order to find "forgiveness", which kept me stuck and in the Hurt phase. Those were the tools and teachings I had at the time, but today I teach acceptance, not forgiveness. We do not need to forgive anyone – not even ourselves; we need to reach radical acceptance and acknowledgement. This is what really sets us free and allows us to heal and move forward with our life. So when I talk about a forgiveness practice, we're really practising acceptance.

I'm all for turning your mess into your message and your superpower, but we need to make sure it's coming from a neutral place of acceptance and not from duality, separation and hierarchy.

It's easy to point the finger and victimize yourself, especially if it involves a severe situation or event. People are often very quick to brand others as narcissists or call them other names online. I've lost count of the amount of breakup posts I've seen where people brand their ex as something or other.

Now, don't get me wrong – but as someone who dated a narcissist who emotionally manipulated me for years, I don't feel the need to tell people about that anymore. It's just another identity, and it doesn't serve anyone. In my view, the term has been overused and only should be used in real situations to educate and create awareness. Naming or shaming someone online does nothing except trap you in victim mode.

Using those sorts of terms to shame someone once again creates duality, separation and hierarchy. While there are people out there who absolutely do come under these descriptions, we can't fall into the prison of judgement over perceived right- and wrongdoing. What they did may be wrong and it did hurt you – all of these things are valid, but it doesn't allow anything to release or heal. Walking away with acceptance and awareness is a much more up-levelled and healed energy to be in.

The way in which we reach radical acceptance is by breaking down our experiences and really witnessing them, so your tasks and actions for this chapter will include more journaling and reflective tasks, which you will find on page 106 at the end of this chapter.

When we look beyond blame and forgiveness, we are challenged to go within and witness the truth of what we're feeling in a non-judgemental process. It may be hard to look past perceived right- or wrongdoings, but these tasks will help you to lean in to that more. No one can fix what happened or change the past, but we can choose to acknowledge the hurt and turn it into acceptance of what was, what is and what will never be. We do this by dropping blame, judgement and hierarchy around ourselves and others.

Dealing with Other People's Negativity

Now, let's talk about something I get asked *a lot* in my work. What should someone do if they are with negative people who keep bringing them down and making them feel negative too? Great question, and I'm sure it's something we've all encountered in our lives. Whether it's an energy vampire, as some people call them, or even a family member, we must protect our energy from their negativity.

Having good energetic hygiene is a must for any Spiritual Queen but it's especially important when we are doing our healing work and find ourselves among negative people. I have a daily energy protection meditation on my YouTube channel (see page 211) which I would highly recommend watching and doing every day if you can. When you cleanse and protect your energy (just like a skincare routine) you allow your thoughts, energy and actions to be your own without external influences.

The truth is, with negative people you just have to let them be negative; there is nothing you can do and it's not your job to fix them either. While it may be frustrating to be around these people regularly, you can't allow them access to your energy. I myself have restricted certain people from accessing my energy and time, because they drained me and I know they didn't have the best intentions. This has included family members who I've stopped playing into it and just let them be. While this may seem harsh, if their company costs you your peace then it's too expensive – and my time and energy is precious to me. I also want to make sure the right people have access to my time and energy who uplift me and feel good to my nervous system, as I'm sure you do too.

We have to drop the judgement, blame and playing into negativity. If you don't like it, don't give these sorts of people access – drop the judgement, protect your energy and let them be too. By doing this, you allow yourself to return to unconditional love and, once again, radical acceptance.

The important thing to do, moving forward, is to witness any judgement, blame or separation that arises. Finding radical acceptance requires patience, witnessing and allowing the unravelling of our layers of hurt to happen when these come up to the surface for healing. When you can change how you see forgiveness, your whole world changes, as you stop pedestalling yourself above someone else, which is the exact opposite of the soul's journey, as this feeds the ego and separates us from oneness.

Other people's actions are their own karma and not something you need to worry about; they played their part as the character they were meant to be in your life, as you did for them too. It's all about the awareness and lessons you take from these events and situations and how you can transform your pain into healing. Stay aware, stay present and come back to this chapter anytime you feel you need this reminder of peace and freedom from the past.

⁺⁺ PRACTICE ⁺⁺

Journaling prompts
- "What else am I feeling alongside this judgement, blame or separation?"
- "What other feelings or emotions lie underneath my response to this situation?"
- "How can I find acceptance with this situation?"

Activity
I would like you to create a judgement list, and on this list I want you to witness where you are judging yourself around this issue. Also, where did those stories come from? If you wish, you could journal using the above prompts and free write around those questions to explore the judgements you are holding on to.

Once you've finished your judgement list, note down anything important you feel could help your healing journey and then destroy this list in a way that feels right to you. I personally feel burning the list is the best way to energetically release it but if you can't safely burn it then please shred, rip up, bury or flush your list. You could also repeat this while destroying your list to help it release:

I witness any judgement I've been holding on to for myself and others. I witness how this judgement, blame and separation are no longer serving me and my journey and ask for my spirit team and the Universe's support to release this from my being and energy. I am ready to release this now and welcome in peace, acceptance and healing for the highest good.

Action
Stay aware, stay present and come back to this chapter anytime you feel you need this reminder of peace and freedom from the past. Be mindful of your judgements and release these as and when you need to. Commit to releasing judgement, blame and feelings of separation. When you create separation from others you also create separation from yourself. How can you come home to yourself and find acceptance and peace with what is?

Surrendering and Letting Go

As with any of your manifestations, letting go and surrendering is the most important and expansive step along the Law of Attraction journey. Before learning true surrender in my life, I will my hold my hands up and admit I was a controller or a "manic manifestor". Along my journey I've truly learned what surrendering to the Universe means and how we can't experience ease and grace in our life without this.

I'm sure some of you will be wondering what happened to the "dream man" I described meeting in Chapter 1 and what that was all about. Well, this book has probably explained a few things already but I didn't know how to have that conversation with myself for a long time, as I felt so much anger. Anger that the relationship didn't work out and also confusion about what it was all for.

This is when, once again, I was being tested by the Universe to learn the lesson of divine surrender and also the lesson of walking away for my highest good. It wasn't an easy journey but it helped me grow, and I thank myself every day for taking that leap of faith and for putting myself and my happiness first.

I was talking about it to my good friend George, who said, "Emma, don't worry about explaining the 'dream man' content to any future partners. It was four years ago, you're an up-levelled version of yourself and a different person, so why wouldn't the dream man up-level too?" When George said this I knew he was right and that I'd been way too hard on myself.

The thing to remember here is that, really, you're not in control. None of us are. Yes, we can set intentions and co-create our reality, but the Universe decides how and when that plays out. Trust in the timing of your life; there are no mistakes. When things feel uncertain anything is possible. Although that thought doesn't always bring much comfort!

Flow into Faith over Fear

COVID-19 taught us all collectively how to slow down and surrender to the unknown. I described at the start of this book how our old lives were stripped away and new ones formed, which changed us all forever. Over this period, we went through many phases and realizations about ourselves and life. Not one person escaped the inevitable change that COVID-19 and the global lockdowns brought us, but ultimately we had to learn to trust in uncertainty, navigate the new reality and even learn to manifest in this new reality. We saw first-hand how we aren't in control and how the collective plan was also in play. Yes, we may be using the Law of Attraction to set our intentions and manifest our heart's desires – but we also need to be aware of other contributing factors.

After deep healing, it can also feel like we're proceeding through a time of uncertainty and a new beginning. This is how I felt each time I up-levelled and closed the doors on those relationships and during the times of COVID-19 too.

Back then, the rug was pulled from underneath us and we were being challenged to adapt, evolve and be present. As we have already seen, change is the only constant we have in this Universe, so flowing into uncertainty with faith over fear is a valuable lesson to add to your spiritual toolkit.

You won't always know why things happen in life; I still don't understand why a lot of events and situations take place and I'm sure you can agree with that too. The thing is that we're not meant to have all the answers: our job is to put our trust and faith in the Universe and the sacred plan.

Things happen all of the time that our human minds can't comprehend but slowly and surely the breadcrumbs will fall into place and guide you to your destiny in line with the sacred plan. We also need to remember that free will, karma, destiny and soul contracts play a part too in how we experience life and our journey.

Trust the Divine Plan

When it comes to my own relationships, I know deep down that things were always meant to unfold in this way purely because of, for example, the synchronicities that were there even before I met my twin flame. When dating new people in more recent years, I've challenged myself not to future trip (see page 111), to be present and to get grounded in this moment. Because that's all we ever truly have.

Maybe we'll have divine assignments that will last a season, maybe a chapter, or maybe even a lifetime – but we have to let go of how we think things should look and surrender to what is. This is one of the hardest lessons for us as humans to grasp – because nothing is ever permanent. Yet when there is no one answer, this means anything is possible.

Yes, we can use our intuition or even go to a psychic to see what our future holds, but the truth is we are the author of our life. What we sense or see when we read other people or ourselves relates to the possibilities that exist within their or our field at that time, as free will means that those timelines and possibilities are ever-changing.

Now, that said, I do believe that some major life events are set in stone and we're always meant to experience these. As souls we create a plan before we come down to Earth, but how we experience those plans is down to us and our free will.

The important thing to remember is that you are always where you're meant to be and you can never do anything wrong because it's exactly how it was supposed to be.

I think we humans can get so tied up in what could have been that we rob ourselves of the joy here and now. Here is your truth: the present is your experience and it's happening now. Stop thinking it could have been any different because that's the ego (and/or your inner child or inner critic) talking.

If you're not happy with an area of your life right now, Queen, you have the power to change that. Never underestimate your incredible power and talent to create your reality. You have free will too, so are you choosing what's for your highest good?

Look for the Gifts in This Moment

Letting go of anything in life can be hard, especially if we've had high hopes for a particular career, relationship, house or friendship, or whatever it may be. Letting go and then walking away can be a relentless process along the spiritual journey, but if something's not vibrating at your level anymore then is it serving you anyway?

Alignment is everything along this journey – especially when it comes to manifesting. It's not about being right, and, oh boy, I think we can all admit when we've wanted to be right. This is why I love these lines from Rumi's poem "Out Beyond Ideas" so much:

Out beyond ideas of wrongdoing

and rightdoing there is a field.

I'll meet you there.

When the soul lies down in that grass

the world is too full to talk about.

When we take ourselves out of a mindset that wants to be right and we no longer focus on outcomes, that is when we witness our gentleness and when we flow. Esther (Abraham) Hicks touches on this when she describes unconditional love as being about caring more about alignment than about being right. The truth is that what is meant for us will never pass us by. So lie down in the field and get present, Queen; you're exactly where you need to be right now.

The present moment is the biggest present we can gift ourselves. When we're living in the past or in the future we can't see clearly, ground ourselves or feel peace. Peace only exists in the present moment – and this means clearing up the past, closing the doors where is needed and accepting it couldn't have been any different.

A tough lesson, I know from my own experiences. Can you sit with how "it couldn't have been any different" feels to you?

Don't Get Lost in Fantasizing about the Future

We saw in Chapter 3 how grief can come in many forms – whether it's about the death of a person or loss in general. This grief over the past or what could have been is called living grief, and I explained how I've had to mourn versions of my life and accept that certain things didn't happen. Many of us stay tangled up in thoughts about what could have been – whether that be a relationship, career, house or friendship. This means that we don't always feel at peace with what is, and that results in the longing and nostalgic feelings of "what if", which can cause yet more anger, depression or feelings of loss.

Another way of spiralling into "what if" happens if we're future tripping and always living in the future. I myself used to be a future tripper, which only ever causes anxiety, disappointment and feelings of uncertainty.

Tomorrow isn't certain, yet many of us spend our lives wishing for and wanting realities that simply aren't happening. Doing this myself kept me stuck, spiralling and miserable, longing for something that was never there in the first place. It stops us from feeling appreciation and gratitude for all we do have and it really zaps the joy out of life.

Because the only moment we ever have is now, the only time your manifestations will come into fruition is in the now. As you can see, neither living in the past nor the future will ever bring you joy – because these mean you're longing for versions of your life that don't exist. Your healing is happening now and your joy can only be found in the now. Your power lies here and now.

Getting Ready to Surrender

There aren't any quick fixes I can give you to help you let go and surrender like a pro; what I've learned over many years of doing this inner work is that there is always more surrendering and letting go to do. Like me, sometimes you'll be able to do these steps with ease and grace, and at other times, the process will bring you to your knees and you'll feel like you're losing a part of yourself. Either way, this is a leaning-in process and must be done authentically to be done properly. Remember, your vibes don't lie!

Letting things be what they need to be is vital in your manifesting journey – you aren't in control and by allowing things to be what they need to be in your life, you allow abundance and what is meant for you to flow to you without resistance. Embodying this is certainly easier said than done, but look at your attachment here; really, the only reason why it's hard to master is because we're fixed on our version of an outcome or manifestation.

What if the Universe has a better plan for you? One that is far grander than you could comprehend – and all that stands in between you and your desire is the fact that you're holding on to a version of your future that doesn't exist?

Let Go of Your Attachment and Resistance

When things feel too much, sometimes it really is a case of coming down on your knees and surrendering; it's about letting go of resistance and whatever it is that you've been trying to hold on to. This can feel intense and like everything is becoming too heavy to carry any longer. The truth is the weight of your attachment is what is really too heavy for you. What would it feel like to put this down?

The first step to true surrendering is to witness the attachment and weight you've been carrying so far. It's also important to remember that everything is energy and when you're attached to an outcome, thinking about it, hoping for it, you're still putting energy toward it. Is there space for the Universe to meet you halfway with this?

If your desire was here, would you be hoping, longing, wishing or wanting – or would you be having fun, living life and grateful for where you're at currently?

If you're struggling to surrender, this means you're not in the present moment – so how can you challenge yourself to just be right now? Be with today, be with yourself, be with your current blessings in life and breathe ...

What is Choosing You Right Now?

Also look at what is currently choosing you; are you choosing yourself? And are you focusing on what is choosing you in life right now, whatever that may be?

We can't choose things that aren't choosing us right now; when we do, this is when we feel the most resistance and attachment. So, catch yourself here and choose what is choosing you today, because this will create the container for more abundance and amazing things to choose you, moving forward. Remember, only want what wants you back! Worry about the rest when it's on the table; for now, choose what's choosing you and the rest will unfold.

The Power of Surrendering

Surrendering is about opening up to all the possibilities and finding peace within that space. It's about knowing that the Universe has heard your desires and wishes, but also trusting that what is for your highest good is unfolding before you. And it always is – we have to remember that.

As much as we try to resist and avoid this, what is meant for us is always unfolding, and we are the ones who make this process harder than it needs to be. When we can detach from an outcome we become true manifesting magnets, but this seems to be the hardest step in all of the manifesting process.

By closing the door on the past, releasing any versions of your future that don't exist either and by grounding yourself in the present moment, you truly become powerful. But keeping the faith throughout this uncertain process can be hard – especially when you're not seeing signs, synchronicities or any evidence in the physical of your manifestation. Personally, I feel that when I kept asking for signs and synchronicities, all along the Universe was really just teaching me how to listen and trust my intuition.

Keep the Faith and Trust Your Intuition

In these powerful moments of new beginnings and next steps into the unknown, it can be hard to know what you want to manifest or your clarity around this may have changed. As we grow and evolve so do our desires, so if in this healing space you want to reflect on and realign your goals then – YASS, Queen – absolutely do this!

When your desires are aligned, faith comes naturally. This doesn't mean you won't have moments where you fear or worry about the materialization of your desires, but faith means you can witness the fear and still ground yourself in knowing and trusting.

Our intuition is our biggest guide here in this lifetime and when you tune into your intuition and trust the signs, feelings and sensations that are communicated to you, you'll be able to witness when your desire is in alignment and whether you're attached to the outcome or still have any expectations around it.

When you tune in and find peace in your answer, you know that's true intuition – but if you tune in and feel anxious and the answer keeps changing, then you know it's a question of attachment and the inner critic, ego or inner child running the show.

Keeping the faith is a process that needs to be leaned in to and one which you may need to repeat a few times when tests or challenges arise, so in those times tune in to the energy of your desire as described above and, remember, if you can sense it, it already exists in the Universe and absolutely can make its way to you when you flow with the sacred plan.

Surrendering your attachment to the outcome may need to be done numerous times, which is why it's important to check in with yourself and your attachment regularly. Are you flowing with the rhythm of life and the natural cycle of your life? Being in a flow state allows you to be truly present each day and find joy here and now. As we saw earlier, when we surrender and let go we also open up our capacity for miracles.

All of your power lies here, in the now, so reclaim it today and know that even in uncertainty you can still manifest your desires through the practice of non-attachment and allowing everything to be as it needs to be in your life without being controlled by your expectations.

How can you drop your expectations around your manifestations and open up to unlimited possibilities instead?

What Does Letting Go Mean?

Surrendering refers to manifesting and letting go of any attachments to an outcome – whereas I see letting go itself as being slightly different. To me, letting go can also mean letting go of the past or of something that's been weighing you down or that feels negative. It could even be letting go of clutter within your home.

Letting go is a pivotal part of the healing process because sometimes we have to let things go so that we are able to welcome in the new. Whether it's friendships that are no longer serving you, relationships, houses, careers, etc., be honest with yourself and identify what drains you or doesn't bring you joy anymore. Only you can answer what you feel comfortable letting go of, but it could even be something emotional you need to let go of as you move through this Healing stage in your journey.

Letting go means that you are shedding the layers of yourself that are no longer needed, including the old version of you and any emotions, energy or pain too. Just like in the surrendering step, we have to make the conscious choice to put the weight down first and realize that we don't have to carry this burden anymore, no matter what it is. There have been a few times in my life when the Universe has pulled the rug from under my feet and I've had no choice but to cry and to let it all come out in order to release the weight and my attachment, or even just to be ready to witness that I need to let something go.

How Do We Let Go and Surrender?

Letting go and surrendering is a liberating step in the Law of Attraction process where we become free from anything holding us back and the shackles of attachment. For some of us, this could simply be about freeing ourselves from attachment to an outcome, while for others of us, we may be finally ready to let go of the past and create space for our abundant future now. It all starts with the choice to put the weight down. So how do we take practical steps to surrender and let go?

First of all, you need to look at your expectations. Yes, I called it so let's be honest here. What expectations have you been putting on yourself or the Universe? Are these healthy expectations or controlling expectations? As we've seen, true surrendering means becoming okay with all outcomes. So are you at peace with all possibilities here or do you feel resistance?

Tune in to how you feel when thinking about all possibilities. Do you feel stubborn and only happy with your outcome, or do you feel open and accepting to all the ways your desires could pan out? Maybe you even need to express some compassion to yourself here if you have put high expectations on yourself and goals. It's okay to witness this because that's heavy too, Queen, and now it's time to put that down for good.

I've got some practical exercises that will help you to surrender and let go, which you'll find at the end of this chapter. Overall, though, this is a reminder for you to get deeply present and grounded. It might also be worth looking at your root chakra (the chakra of grounding and stability) or your solar plexus (the chakra of inner power and confidence) and seeing if you need to balance them through meditation, as these are the two chakras that most often get out of balance when someone is resisting surrendering and letting go.

You could also repeat this powerful affirmation daily:

I take back my power.

We give away our power so easily, both consciously and unconsciously on a daily basis, so repeating this mantra can help to balance the solar plexus and also help you to naturally surrender and let go.

The real reason you're struggling to let go and surrender is because you feel like it's out of your power. While, yes, some aspects of our lives and manifestations always will be beyond our power, there is still so much that is in your control in every given moment. You choose how you feel, Queen, and you can choose whether you stay attached and weighed down or surrendered and at peace.

So, after looking at your expectations and dropping any that are unrealistic or unhealthy for yourself and the Universe to deliver, it's time to reclaim your power here in the now. You have the power to change this and release this weight. Drop it, Queen, you don't need to carry this anymore.

✦✦ PRACTICE ✦✦

Journaling prompts
- "What would it feel like to put down these expectations?"
- "How can I challenge myself to 'just be' right now?"

Activity
First of all, you're going to write an honest letter to yourself or the Universe, or just jot down sentences on a piece of paper if you prefer. (Extra points if you can do this on a full moon.) You're going to write down what you're ready to release and let go of now. What weight are you ready to put down? What are you ready to say "fuck it" to and release?

After you've written down everything, I want you to find a bucket in your home and name it the "Fuck It Bucket". This bucket is for you to throw all your attachment, frustration or anger into. When you are ready, scrunch up the note with your sentences or your letter on and throw this into your Fuck It Bucket, confirming to the Universe you are ready to let this go now and no longer need to carry this weight.

Once you're done, take your paper and destroy this in a heat-proof container. You can then burn your paper safely and once again affirm that you're letting this weight and burden go now. If you can't burn the paper, please shred it, bury it in soil, rip it up or flush it down the toilet.

Next, you're going to write a gratitude list for all the blessings and happiness you have in your life currently. This is a powerful practice that will help you to get grounded and present in the now.

Structure your gratitude sentences as follows "I am so grateful for ... because ...". Write down as many points as you can and read each point out afterwards, finishing with the words "thank you, thank you, thank you, Universe".

Keep this list safe so you can reflect on it when you need a reminder of the wonderful things happening here and now.

You're then going to set the intention that for today you're not going to worry about the future or the outcome, and tomorrow you can pick these back up if you choose to. But for today you're going to choose not to worry about this and dedicate your day to yourself, fun and joy.

Action

Your action for "Surrendering and Letting Go" is to do an angelic cord-cutting meditation to once again release any negative attachment to your desires. You can find one on my *Hurt, Healing, Healed* meditation playlist (see page 211). This will help you to release control and let you naturally surrender.

If you are really feeling the intensity and resistance to letting go, I invite you to allow the Universe to bring you to your knees. This is the deepest surrender practice you can do. Get down on your knees and allow yourself to cry, feel the emotions and any resistance as it comes to the surface. Allow your body to release the energy and sit with your emotions for as long as you need to; you will start to feel lighter and that you can naturally hand this issue over to the Universe now and trust you are supported with it.

Bonus activity

Look up Brad Yates on YouTube and try his "Letting Go and Surrendering" EFT video to help instantly release any intense emotions from your meridian points (your energetic centres).

Self-care, Self-love and Self-worth

In my previous book, *Positively Wealthy*, I shared the importance of self-love and how vital it is to have a solid self-care routine and relationship with yourself. Looking back on my healing journey and as you continue yours in this book, I've reflected upon the steps to reaching real self-worth and how we can truly embody unconditional love for our self. Remember that you can't truly love anything external unconditionally until you find peace and love within yourself first. We must always do the inner work first to receive and experience love and joy in our outer experience.

Many people may believe self-love is vain or a waste of time but having a happy healthy relationship with yourself is what brings peace, happiness and acceptance. So as we embark on the last healing chapter of Part Two, I want to share with you what the differences between self-care, self-love and self-worth are and why they form three separate stages. I honestly feel if every human had the awareness and access to these tools and knowledge the world would be a much happier space. Now more than ever we need to come back home to ourselves and love the skin we're in to find fulfilment and abundance in our life ...

Before we begin, I want you to check in with yourself and ask yourself on a scale of 1 to 10 (1 being "I don't love myself" and 10 being "I love myself, I'm Beyoncé") where would you rate yourself on the self-love scale today? If you're struggling with this question tune in and trust the first number that comes up.

Many people seek self-love and self-worth but don't realize this is a journey and a process – you can't just skip to having healthy self-worth without first cultivating self-care and self-love. They may feel it's impossible to feel love for their self, which is why we're going to start at the beginning with self-care.

Self-care

Self-care is the physical implementation and actions each week that embody self-love. So these are practical things you do for yourself to show yourself that you care and value yourself.

To build a loving and healthy relationship with yourself during healing or maybe even for the first time in your life, you have to start off with this foundational step of self-care. Right now, it may feel like a massive leap to love yourself or love yourself fully, so we're going to start off with the basics.

Each week it's really important that you follow a balanced routine to help cultivate self-care through loving actions, but in order to do this you must first create the space. Once a week from now on, no matter how busy your life gets, I want you to dedicate an evening or a morning or an afternoon to yourself. Call it the "[Your name] evening or day".

Once a week you're going to do the following three-step self-care routine and you can journal in your notebook what you'd like to do for each step this week:

1. **Do something for yourself,** whether this is writing a self-love list (see page 129), reading a good self-help book, pampering yourself, listening to a podcast or doing something that will bring you great joy. Make sure that once a week you do something for yourself by yourself that will fill your own cup of happiness.

2. **Treat yo' self!** Whether it be the new dress you've been lusting over, your favourite chocolate, a night out, some flowers or simply something you've been saving up for. The goal here isn't how much money you can spend, it's about the joy and good feeling that item will bring

to your day. No matter how big or small, make sure you treat yourself to something that will bring you joy this week.

3. **Do something socially to bring you joy.** Whether with your friends, family or partner, do something fun once a week to socialize and enjoy the moment. If you're single, you could make it your date night each week and go out with friends to "create" space for that special someone to come into your life.

Make sure that you stick to these three steps at least once a week and see what healing miracles start to take place in your life, Queen. Take note of how your relationship with yourself improves over the course of the Healing and Healed stages and how your external relationships also begin to change as a result of this.

Self-love

Now that you have a solid self-care routine in place that you're going to implement moving forward, notice how it makes you feel to be taking loving action for yourself and carving out the time for your beautiful self.

Next, it's time to build your relationship with yourself. While self-care focuses on external physical actions, self-love focuses on your one-to-one relationship with yourself and how you view or speak about yourself. Self-love is sanity and there is nothing wrong with taking charge of your life and putting yourself first; this is the first sign of healing – that you witness and acknowledge your needs and what will bring you peace and happiness.

Below, I'll be sharing some great practices to help you nurture a loving and harmonious relationship with yourself which can then be built up to the self-worth stage. But first of all, I want to talk about pleasure as this is a big factor in the self-love journey. So many people are switched off from the fun in life (which I covered earlier on in Chapter 6, "Connecting with Your Inner Child") and pleasure.

Pleasure is about deeply enjoying the experiences and even little tasks in life. If you were to rate how much pleasure you experience in day-to-day life (with 0 per cent being "none" and 100 per cent being "I experience full pleasure everyday") where would you rate your pleasure currently?

Pleasure comes down to two things: feeling happiness and enjoyment with all you do and how much you love yourself and body. YASS, we're talking sexy pleasure but also inner child pleasure in terms of fulfilment in everyday life. How do you feel about your body? How do you feel about your sensuality and sexual organs?

Having a healthy and pleasurable relationship with your body and self not only allows you to embody self-love but also allows you to become a magnet for abundance in many forms. When we feel sexy and full of love we feel happy – and happiness creates joy and joy creates a vibration of abundance. So not only will pleasure bring you many rewards internally, it will also help to cultivate the dream life you seek, which is full of pleasure, joy and fulfilment. To embody those emotions that relate to your desires, you must create those feelings within you through all forms of pleasure. So that everyday you're inviting in pleasure in whatever way feels good to you.

The reason why so many people lack self-love is because society has taught us it's egotistical and wrong. So many of us have such a disconnection to ourselves, bodies and pleasure because of this. Even if you're reading this and thinking "Hey Emma, I've been doing self-love for years!", it's still possible to let it slip over time – especially after the pandemic affected all our lives – and maybe this is the very reminder you need to fully embody self-love in your life.

Self-love Affirmations

A great way to get started with self-love is to work with your mirror. Too often we breeze past the mirror when getting ready in the morning or when brushing our teeth but looking in it is actually one way we can connect with ourselves easily.

So first of all, I want you to stand or sit in front of your mirror and see how you feel looking into your eyes. Notice what comes up for you as you sit with yourself and give yourself this time. Now I'd like you to repeat an affirmation.

Many people enjoy working with affirmations and I really like to include these in self-love practices. The most important part of working with any affirmations is that they feel believable to you. You can't expect an affirmation that feels like a 1 or 2 on the belief scale to work or feel good. Even with the Law of Attraction everything starts with a level of belief.

So rate your affirmations on a scale of 1 to 10 (1 being "I don't believe" and 10 being "I fully believe"). If your affirmation is a 7 or above it's safe to work with this. If it's a 6 or below, simplify the affirmation to something that does feel a 7 or above for you. In time as you repeat the simplified affirmation when it feels like a 9 or a 10 then you can upgrade it to the original affirmation as this will feel higher on the scale by that point. Make sure to mix up your affirmations regularly to keep them fun and exciting.

For the next 21 days I want you to repeat a few self-loving affirmations in the mirror each day alongside your weekly self-care routine (which hopefully you'll do each and every week forever more). Write down your self-love score and affirmation scores at the beginning of your 21 days and then check in after the 21 days to see how they have improved and how you're feeling as a whole.

You can create your own self-love affirmations but here are a few examples to get you started:

- "I love and approve of myself."
- "I love you (your own name)."
- "I am worthy and deserving of love."
- "I am beautiful inside and out."
- "I am worthy of my time and love."
- "I am beautiful and kind."
- "I love and honour myself."
- "I am surrounded by love and acceptance."
- "I have compassion and patience with myself."
- "It's safe for me to love and respect myself."
- "I respect myself and know I am doing my best."
- "I listen to my needs and honour these every day."

Show Yourself Compassion

Next up, to take this self-love to the next level, it's time to look at two more areas – compassion and the heart chakra.

As souls in human form, we are often extremely critical and hard upon ourselves, again because of the outside world and what we're taught when growing up. Compassion is something many struggle to find for themselves although we can often easily express compassion for others. Why is this? I believe it's because it's easier to sympathize and forgive someone else than to do that with ourselves. We hold ourselves to such high expectations that when we don't meet them we feel shame, blame, regret or even embarrassment. You are human, I am human we are all going to mess up and get it wrong sometimes.

A true element of self-love is having compassion for yourself and nurturing that through the language you use with yourself. Instead of beating yourself up over something, how can you gently reassure and nurture yourself instead? Rather than holding something against yourself, how can you see yourself through the eyes of love and compassion?

If a friend or loved one came to you with the same issue, what would you say to them? Would you have a go at them and shame them, or would you hug them, show them compassion and give them reassurance? You too deserve the love you so freely give to others. So remind yourself that you are worthy and deserving of compassion too. When we extend compassion to ourselves, we can then build ourselves up in an aligned, healthy way rather than traumatizing ourselves further.

Connect with Your Heart Chakra

Our heart chakra is also another key element in our self-love and healing journey. According to the spiritual teachings most familiar in the West, there are seven main chakras within our energetic body (which exists a few inches outside of our physical body), and our heart chakra is located in the middle of our chest just to the right of our physical heart.

This energetic space is the key to a lot of the healing we'll be doing within this book so you'll be working with this particular chakra a lot throughout these chapters. If you've never worked with your heart chakra before then take some time to do some research online into the chakras and place your hand on your heart chakra and tune into it – how does it make you feel?

The heart chakra is all about giving and receiving love, so when the chakra is balanced and open this means you have a healthy relationship with self-love and are able to give and receive love in equal measure. When the chakra is blocked, stagnant or underactive, this may mean that you've been giving away too much love and not receiving it, or, vice versa, you've been receiving openly but not giving love in equal measure. You can also have an over-active heart chakra where you've been going above and beyond again with an unbalanced giving and receiving of love.

To fully embody unconditional love, we have to have a healthy and balanced relationship with giving and receiving love – which means working with your heart chakra is a great place to start when it comes to self-love!

For your self-love task, I want you to write a self-love list, which you'll find described at the end of this chapter. If you did this is when reading *Positively Wealthy*, it's time to check in with this again as I've added in some extras. Use this exercise as a starting point with your self-love journey, which you can come back to at any point. Keep your list safe and add to it whenever you wish, or write a new list when you feel called to. This exercise doesn't have to been done regularly but I would encourage you to keep up the mirror work for 21 days after this exercise – whether it's repeating the "I love you" statement to yourself daily or one of the other affirmations listed on page 123.

Some other ways you can help to balance and open your heart chakra is by working with colours and crystals. The heart chakra is a beautiful emerald green colour so any green clothing or food will be great for working with the heart chakra. You could wear a green scarf or garment or even make a super-yummy green smoothie or green salad bowl – whatever you feel drawn to!

Crystals I recommend working with to help balance the heart chakra include green jade, emerald, rose quartz, green adventurine, malachite and amazonite. You can wear these crystals and have them on you throughout the day to promote positive energy and balancing, or you could place them on your heart chakra and meditate with them.

You can listen to my heart chakra meditation to accompany this chapter by visiting the link on page 211. The meditation is designed to help you balance and align your heart chakra during the healing process. Try this meditation out and come back to it as often as you need to. As with all meditation, take what feels good and resonates with you, and discard anything that doesn't. If it's your first time meditating, go with the flow and allow the images to appear as they need to. Even if you just see colours or fall asleep the healing still works, so don't worry!

You could also work with a heart chakra aura spray (available to purchase online and in New Age stores) to clear and charge your energy.

Other great ways to continue developing self-love include praising yourself often and spending quality time with yourself. It's not usually enough just to spend an evening watching Netflix alone – although if that's your act of self-care, great! But look at the *quality* time you are spending with yourself and how nurturing and enriching that time really is. You deserve quality time with yourself, Queen, and you deserve to be gentle and kind to yourself too.

Self-worth

As you embody the last and final step of self-love – self-worth – it's important that you know exactly what this means. Self-worth means knowing you are worthy and deserving of love, abundance and all the wonderful things this Universe has to offer. It's about implementing healthy and loving boundaries with yourself and others and taking loving action if need be, to honour your worth.

Self-worth has been the biggest step for me to achieve, because I wasn't fully embodying self-care and self-love first of all. For nine years I sacrificed my self-worth for relationships that ended anyway, I didn't stand up for myself and I didn't honour my needs. This resulted in a disconnection to unconditional love, myself and my body, creating a spiral of self-hate and self-sabotage.

When I finally learned about self-worth and tried to implement this, I would shout from the rooftops to try and get the respect I deserved from my relationships, but, see, real self-worth is a vibe – it's an energy. It was my inner child that felt the need to voice these boundaries, thinking that this was true self-worth. But real self-worth and healthy boundaries aren't about shouting them from the rooftops in the hope someone will respect you. Knowing your worth and boundaries means you can lovingly navigate life, while peacefully knowing you can walk your talk if you ever need to. You don't need to voice your boundaries for someone to get them, so heal that part of yourself, Queen.

True self-worth is the embodiment of energy while having the grace to trust the Universe is protecting you. I had to check in with this myself recently. After doing so much work on self-worth over the years and finally reaching a place where my energy brought in the most loving and respectful man into my life, I noticed I still had a pattern where I would voice a boundary even if it wasn't being tested. I knew this was my survival identity, which had got me through the last nine years, and I realized now that it was safe to trust and know that the right people won't need you to tell them about your boundaries because they'll already love and respect you enough to know them.

What held me stuck in my previous relationship for so long was my lack of self-worth. I kept choosing that reality and hoping it would magically get better. I gave it my all, every last ounce of energy, until I woke up and recognized I'd scarified my physical health, mental health, energy and three years of my life and I was still being constantly disrespected – because I held no respect for myself.

Although I did self-care each week and loved myself and my body, I allowed that relationship to play out far longer than I should have. I kept wishing for an alternative reality and for the relationship to magically fix itself or for someone else even better to walk in – but how could the Universe do that when I was choosing my not-very-abundant reality time and time again? At the time it didn't feel like I was choosing it, of course. I was desperate for change and a miracle, but every time I allowed the same sorts of things to happen, stayed quiet or didn't walk, I was choosing that reality.

In the Law of Attraction, you're taught that you are choosing the reality you're experiencing now – which for me didn't feel true, until I could witness how I wasn't embodying self-worth at all. People would try to tell me this and that my sacral chakra was constantly imbalanced – and I still couldn't see it.

But at the right time I did and I knew I deserved so much better. Dates came along after this who were more aligned to what I wanted in a partner, but again I was challenged and had to walk my talk and know I deserved better. Finally, when I knew my self-worth was truly embodied and I didn't feel scared of walking away from people and things anymore, the right people who naturally and effortlessly respected me did come into my life – it was as easy as breathing. My nervous system felt calm and when I met my current partner I knew he valued and respected me fully because we both respected ourselves.

So my message to you is that if you're not happy in your current circumstances you can absolutely change them, but you must embody your self-worth first and know you deserve more. Embodied self-worth will give you the awareness and confidence to walk away from anything no longer serving you and welcome in what can and will serve you for the highest good. It all starts with action, and self-worth is a very actionable step as well as an energetic one. Your energy attracts your reality, after all!

Work with Your Chakras

Another great way to embody your self-worth is by working with your solar plexus chakra. The solar plexus chakra is located at the top of your stomach and is bright sunshine yellow in colour. This chakra represents power, worth and confidence, so making sure this chakra is balanced is key when working on self-worth. And it may be helpful to look into the sacral chakra too. This is at the bottom of your stomach or womb space if you have one. The sacral chakra is a beautiful orange in colour and represents pleasure, sensuality, sexuality and creativity. Very often with issues around self-worth, you'll find these two chakras are out of balance, alongside the heart chakra.

A great way to honour yourself and action your self-worth is to tune in to your body when making decisions. Real self-worth is knowing when to say yes and when to say no. If it's not feeling like a hell YASS then it's a hell no, but more often than not, people with low self-worth are inclined to people-please and go against their own intuition or needs, so it's time to honour those needs. This will allow you to reclaim you power and have a healthy and nurturing relationship with yourself, full of unconditional love.

⁺⁺ PRACTICE ⁺⁺

Journaling prompts
- "What can I do this week to tick off all three steps in my self-care routine?"
- "What does self-care mean to me?"

Activity
In your journal or notebook you're going to write an honest list with all the things you love about yourself. This could be statements such as "I love how creative I am" or "I love my long legs"; the only catch is they must be true statements. This is not what you want to love about yourself – these statements must feel real to you here and now.

Challenge yourself to connect to your heart chakra during this task. Tune in to what you love about yourself with your heart charka and see what sensations or emotions come up for you.

Once you've finished your list, you're going to take this to the mirror and read out each point while looking into your eyes. If it helps to place your hand on your heart chakra too, then please do so. Once you've finished reading out each point I want you to seal the practice by saying "I love you, [your name]" while looking into your eyes.

Action
A great way to honour yourself and action your self-worth is to tune in to your body when making decisions. When you're asked out by your friends, or your boss at work asks you to stay on late again, and you really don't want to, it's about voicing your needs and wants in a loving way, making sure to honour yourself and what is a hell YASS or a hell no for you. Make sure to practise this in day-to-day life as the first step to truly embodying self-worth is being able to speak up with love and honouring yourself authentically.

Bonus activity
Remember to do my heart chakra meditation, which you can find on page 211.

Healing FAQ

In this chapter, I would like to answer some of the questions I frequently get asked on my platforms and in my coaching sessions to help you along your healing journey. Of course, if anything else comes up for you that I haven't answered below I have a ton of free content on my channels to help and guide you. Please also refer to the Resources section at the end of the book for useful books, information and people you can work with to help with anything that may arise.

What is a healing crisis?

A healing crisis can happen after a healing or coaching session with someone or even when you are exploring your own healing. Sometimes when we uncover healing to be done, these wounds can feel more potent or worse for a few days afterwards. This is completely normal and will usually last for a maximum of five to seven days. During this time, make sure to keep up your self-love and self-care rituals. I'd also recommend adding Epsom salt to your bubble bath to help clear the heavy energy. The worst thing you can do is sit still when you're feeling triggered or in a healing crisis, so make sure to move the energy through you in a healthy way that feels good to you. Although a healing crisis can feel like it's made everything worse, this is a positive sign that the emotions are coming up to be released and normally within 48 hours you will start to see things shift and feel more peaceful and lighter again. Once the healing crisis has past you will usually notice the original trigger won't feel as prominent anymore.

What is collective energy?

Collective energy refers to the energy of the globe, including all of us human beings. You may hear teachers or gurus referring to the collective energy, and how we can affected by it. Collective energy can impact us individually and even affect our moods and energy. That's why when you're triggered it's so important to feel into whether this energy is yours to carry or not. If it feels like your stuff and triggering you emotionally then it's definitely yours to witness and work on. If, however, it feels uncomfortable but it doesn't feel triggering or like it's shaking you then more than likely this is collective energy at play. When you are impacted by collective energy you can set an intention with the Universe to help clear this so you can feel your true energy and emotions. Imagine a white angelic protective bubble surrounding you fully and say, "I call upon my Angels and the Universe to please clear and transmute any energy from my aura, energetic field or within me that isn't mine to carry or that stops me from being my happy authentic self. Thank you, thank you, thank you, Universe, and so it is."

Is the moon or astrology affecting me?

Nine times out of ten the answer is yes! Whether it's a potent full moon challenging us to release and look at old beliefs or wounds, or a planet in retrograde like Mercury slowing us down and making us feel heavy and exhausted, the moon and planetary system can absolutely have an effect on our moods, energy and emotions. Think about it – we're made up of water so just like the ocean is affected by the moon, we are too. This is why I always sit with anything that comes up for me or feels intense for a few days. I do what I can to support myself and allow it to pass through. In the same way, if a situation comes up around a new or full moon, during the eclipse season, equinox or solstice or planetary retrograde, try to tune in and see if it's yours to work with or not. Sit with it for a few days and if it still feels potent then that's when you know it's time to book in with someone and get help or do inner work and reflection yourself.

What is purging?

Purging is something that happens to our physical and emotional bodies when we purge emotions and energy through healing. This can manifest in so many different ways for each person but most typically when doing deep healing you may experience flu symptoms, a cold, diarrhoea, vomiting, headaches or chills afterwards during the healing crisis. These are just a few examples I've experienced and seen with clients over the years; these are also ascension symptoms (signs that we are up-levelling) but will feel like a spiritual illness as you witness and feel old energy purging quite literally from you. Again, there is nothing to worry about with this; our bodies are intelligent and will intuitively guide us to anything we may need to support our system – and it's always better out than in! Remember that energy and emotions have to leave one way or another and this will soon pass and you'll feel even lighter and happier afterwards. Of course, if any of these symptoms persist for more than 72 hours please do seek medical advice for peace of mind.

Why does the same wound keep coming up?

Remember that healing is like working through the layers of an onion, so when wounds or fears come up this doesn't mean you've failed or haven't done the work. This is a common misconception with healing and it's important to remember that a new layer is not a negative, as the layers will become lighter and easier to work through each time.

How will I know when I'm healed?

You'll know you're healed by the way you feel. While the healing journey is lifelong, you can see your limiting beliefs and fears dissolve with time and positive action. The best way to judge your healing is by your comeback rate – not by the thoughts that come up. Thoughts will arise; we're only human and have thousands of thoughts a day. The real way to track your healing is by how the thoughts make you feel. If you're feeling less triggered and fazed by the same thought or fear then this is a sure sign that you're working on the layers and doing a great job. So keep going and remember it's all about how you feel within you that's the real scale of success.

Should I take medication and speak to my doctor if it feels too much?

Please let me reassure you that there is nothing to be ashamed of in turning to Western medicine if you feel you need it. Some people, for example, have a chemical imbalance that impacts their emotions and moods, so they may need professional medical help to manage this. Receiving help is not a sign of weakness and it is also a spiritual act. I myself have turned to modern medicine when I've needed it and there's certainly a time and place for it. So please always do speak to your local doctor or healthcare professional for support and to consider your options. If anything ever feels too much then it's definitely a good idea to get some support. You can also look into supplements and working with a nutritionist, or other alternative ways to help boost your internal health, energy and moods if you don't want to take pharmaceutical medications. If you are looking to go down an alternative route, please ensure you are working with a trained therapist, counsellor or coach to support you during this time. Mental health issues are nothing to be ashamed of, and the more we have open honest conversations about how we're really feeling and support ourselves and others in getting help, the sooner we will all understand that there is a time and place for everything. Admitting we need help can be a powerful step in our healing journey.

Healing Check-in

Once you've completed the tasks and actions in Part Two, journal on the questions below either here or in a notebook of your choice.

What are your biggest takeaways from this section?

_____

_____

_____

What three things are you going to implement from this section?

_____

_____

_____

What have you discovered within yourself through reading and working with Part Two: Healing?

_____

_____

_____

What healing modalities do you feel drawn to explore?

_____

_____

_____

What areas of your life do you feel will benefit from this healing work?

_____

_____

_____

How can you commit to inner child work, moving forward?

_____

_____

_____

How can you re-parent yourself and heal your inner child?

_____

_____

How can you flow more with life and with your healing?

_____

_____

_____

What does your body need from you right now?

_____

_____

_____

Rating Scale

In the table below, circle your score from 1 to 10 for each quality (with 1 being extremely unhappy and 10 being very happy).

Happiness:	1	2	3	4	5	6	7	8	9	10
Self-love:	1	2	3	4	5	6	7	8	9	10
Fulfilment:	1	2	3	4	5	6	7	8	9	10
Self-worth:	1	2	3	4	5	6	7	8	9	10
Confidence:	1	2	3	4	5	6	7	8	9	10
Gratefulness:	1	2	3	4	5	6	7	8	9	10

Total   =   /60

PART THREE:
Healed

"Beautiful are those whose brokenness gives birth to transformation and wisdom."

John Mark Green

Now that you have embarked on a deeply transformational healing journey in Part Two and faced your shadow, it's time to embody this experience and meet the new Healed version of yourself. In Part Three, you will embody all of the beautiful healing work you've been doing so far and reconnect back fully to unconditional love.

I will guide you through this with my manifestation processes and show you how to align with abundance and your desires from this Healed space and how to become your most abundant happiest self now that you're free from the past and previous blocks.

By the end of Part Three, you will feel fully empowered and ready to welcome in your wildest dreams, having fully reclaimed your power. You will also be ready to become the Spiritual Queen you always dreamed of being, feeling at peace and in alignment with yourself and the Universe, and experiencing ease and flow in your life and with your manifestations.

Meeting the New You

After reaching the Healed space (which is of course a continuous journey in itself) it's time to meet this new version of yourself. When you reach this stage, it can feel like uncharted waters. As exciting as new beginnings and prospects feel, you will also have to have the courage to step forward and claim this new version of yourself.

Over the course of the last few years, I've met countless new versions of myself, which at the time felt in alignment with my higher self – but we are designed to continue to evolve and grow during our time here. I know when I first spiritually awakened, I wanted to meet a more authentic and honest version of myself. As I've grown over the years, I found myself walking more into authenticity and giving myself permission to fiercely be who I am deep down.

For so long I was serious in my personal life and career, yet after discovering inner child work and healing I wanted to allow my sense of humour to come through and share my cheeky side more often. I wanted to show the world the version of me who loves to dance, laugh, eat cake, make inappropriate jokes, share my embarrassing stories and the version of me who isn't perfect and never has been.

It's strange, when you're in the public eye you feel like people can pedestal you and see you as this perfect being – when in reality, when people get to know me and see my humour and imperfectness online, they see the *real* Emma.

As confident and determined as I am in my work, in my personal life I can actually be quite nervous and shy. Around the right people this soon disappears but in order to be able to completely express who I am, I have had to love myself unconditionally.

To fully be seen and loved for my authentic self, I first had to turn up as that version of myself. I needed to be brave and I understand that some people wouldn't want to see an imperfect human being turn up in their work and life. But actually, what happened was that a ton of joy, abundance, love and magic was created as I explored the new me.

So don't be afraid if this is how you feel now in this stage; or maybe you've felt this recently and feel like you've evolved again already. This will happen and all it takes is for you to give yourself permission to show up as your true self.

So many of us hide our real essence, our funny quirks or silly sense of humour but guess what – we need that in the world! So many of us suppress the inner child and want to be serious, like I once did.

I also suppressed my sense of humour and sensuality for a long time in fear men would think I was too forward, too sexual, not "feminine" enough – but ladies, I know we've all felt this and the right partner will *love* all these qualities in you. I'd been shamed for some comments I'd made in the past by a guy I dated and my good friend Hannah reminded me, "Emma, most men *would want* to hear you say you want to rip their clothes off!" For weeks I shamed and blamed myself for making that comment when he asked if I was sexually attracted to him, so to receive a rejection felt awful and as if all the hard work I'd done to feel confident around men and be my true self after trauma suddenly didn't feel enough again. I then had to revisit the pattern and realize that it was healed, I wasn't regressing and that actually I had done all I could – and saying something like that isn't a crime when you're dating someone, it's a compliment.

Take the Time to Get to Know the New You

Allowing yourself to be your true weird self is beautiful – but sometimes we have to work to uncover that self.

A good friend of mine who has suffered with depression for many years had gone through a recent crisis and he explained how after therapy and medication he didn't know who he was anymore. He was happier but he had lost all he was. I explained how the version of himself from before was gone, it wasn't serving him and he was this new version of himself now. A new one that needed exploring, nurturing and compassion.

We are so quick to judge ourselves and think we have to have things all figured out – but in reality no one has everything figured out at the beginning and maybe never at all.

When you don't know who you are anymore it's time to create the person that you want to be. It's a calling – an initiation from the Universe to say claim who you want to be now, fearlessly. This is an awakening where you can look at what wasn't working and what you can do to become who you want to be. There is no rush in this process; it's an unfolding. For my friend, it was still very early days but I know he felt the pressure as a man to have it all figured out.

We also have to allow ourselves to honour what we need. The first step in meeting this new version of yourself is to honour what you need in any moment. Start off small by enquiring each day, "What do I need today?" Little by little, every day, as you honour yourself and your needs in the moment, eventually you'll get to a place where you start discovering yourself again and feel more like yourself – but a new version. There isn't a magical way to suddenly know yourself fully and completely; it's a process of unravelling and feeling into it. Just like a caterpillar, we shed our old identity as we go into the cocoon.

Embrace the Change

It's funny when you bump into people from your past and they comment, "Oh, you've changed!" Well what did they expect? The healing process is transformative and as we grow and evolve, of course our personality does too – our likes, dislikes and passions all change as we do.

Yet we can attach to our old identities. To give you an example of this, because of the trauma and negative relationships I'd experienced one after the other, my identity used to be trauma. I didn't know a life without trauma. So when I went on the healing journey described in this book I initially felt lost because I didn't know who I was here and now without the trauma, without the limiting beliefs and without the desire for codependent relationships. I had no clue what life looked like without trauma.

I won't lie – it took some time to adjust to this new healed feeling. It was fun and expansive discovering who I was without trauma, but when something has been ingrained in you for so long, meeting the new you requires you to shed these old identities and form new healed and positive ones here and now. So don't worry if you feel like you're still changing or are scared right now; it does feel scary and like a Band-Aid has been ripped off when you re-enter the world healed. Think of the trauma, or whatever it was, as being like your old comfort blanket which you don't need anymore – I promise the new you and what's waiting for you don't require you to play it safe anymore. Reassure your inner child of this too!

Be Proud of How Far You Have Come

It's also important to be proud of yourself and how far you've come. Being a human and doing the inner work isn't easy and it isn't always pretty but the peace and love we feel from doing it is worth every moment of previous discomfort.

In coaching sessions, I often set the task of writing an achievement list where I get the client to list every achievement and moment in life that has made them feel proud. But for this chapter, I want to take it even deeper and make this juicer for you. I want you to write an appreciation list too. But instead it's going to be a list of all the moments you've overcome and grown from, and it could be moments you're really proud of too. So your list could look like this:

- I am proud of the time I went to therapy and opened up to receive healing.
- I am proud of the time I walked away from a toxic relationship.
- I am proud of myself for witnessing my wrong doings in that relationship and working on them.
- I am proud of being vulnerable and opening up to love again after being hurt.

I love this practice because it allows you to really go deep and witness all the achievements in your life that may not look like awards or public recognition, etc., but were actually about healing and overcoming the very things we came here to experience in this life. We all need to witness how brave and strong we are to navigate life's uncertainties and choose better after adversity because that takes real guts and courage to do, Queen!

Accept That You Are Perfectly Imperfect

This practice leads me nicely onto the third step in meeting this new version of yourself after healing: acknowledging that you're going to get it wrong. You're going to mess up, learn and grow even more – but now you have the awareness.

We all need to show up imperfectly and accept that no one is perfect. It's dangerous when we pedestal ourselves or others as we can fall off that pedestal as quickly as we were put on it. When you allow yourself to show up authentically and as you need to, other people's expectations become their own problem – not yours.

I was always told the famous saying that "it's better to show up imperfectly than not at all" and I couldn't agree more. Being an ex-perfectionist (it really is a continuous journey un-conditioning this trait), I would often have rather not shown up at all. After numerous times of trying to be perfect in relationships and life, I realized it wasn't getting me anywhere as I wasn't being my authentic, messy, human self! The divine feminine energy is very messy and as I began to embody this more, I realized that it was okay not to be perfect; that I probably was going to say or do the wrong things but I had new awareness, perspective and the knowledge that you can't fuck up what's meant for you.

How beautiful is it when we can be fully seen as our messy selves in our connections and relationships – and still be loved and held! This is what I had been lacking for years and relaxing into this knowledge and space allowed me to realize being myself *was* safe.

I think the reason why so many people hide their beautiful authentic self is because it feels safe – it feels safe in a world that has been conditioned by perfection and unrealistic expectations. Well, Queen, I'm here to tell you to burn the rule book – burn it and never look back. Suppressing the true you is exhausting and a waste of this precious time.

We are on this planet for such a short amount of time and you don't want to get to the end of this all and say, "Oh, all that time I hid my true to self to suit everyone else's comfort zones"; you want to say, "I showed up as my true self and had a blast. I showed others it was safe for them to be their true self too and we all allowed one another to be seen and held unconditionally." Maybe it's a big wish for us to see everyone burn the rule book and embody their true self in this lifetime but a Spiritual Queen can dream, right?!

Who Will You Inspire Today?

Think about who you could inspire by being your true self today. Think about who you could also inspire to heal and step into their true power. This path isn't always the easiest – being a maverick takes strength and commitment to yourself and your values. There will be judgement from others who feel scared of your light – but love them anyway. There will be people who question your choices and maybe put you down out of projection and fear – but love and respect them anyway and still be you. No one should tell you how to live your life or who you should be. YOU get to decide that for yourself.

So, use this new beginning as the very invitation to claim all you know in your soul – all you are and can be. Tell a guy you want to rip his clothes off because one day the right one will be like, "Hell YASS please!" Tell someone your loving boundaries and implement them. Dress and be who you have always wanted to be. If you've always wanted to travel – do it! If you've always wanted to learn a new language or skill – do it! Being your true self is sexy in many ways energetically, physically and emotionally and I mean sexy in a whole body YASS way for yourself.

As Rumi, one of my favourite poets, said, "Tear off the mask. Your face is glorious." Your face *is* glorious, Queen, and life is too short to not do the things you love. Too many people take dreams and goals to the grave without these having ever seen the daylight. Don't let your dreams and true self die within you – let them shine eternally and be expressed fully in this lifetime.

The New You and Manifesting

In terms of how all this ties into manifestation – remember that everything is energy. When we hide our true self and suppress our authentic expression of that self, how can we vibe with the version of ourselves who has that desire? The version of you who has that desire is going to be happy, joyful and living their best life, right? So how can you live your best life here and now? How can you become the version of yourself who has that desire?

Giving yourself permission to express your true messy self is beautiful and allows you to receive. It allows you to be present and brings fulfilment. Remember, your desires will always be fulfilled when you need them the least – so don't wait for your desires to give you permission to meet this new version of yourself.

Meet yourself now and allow your desires to come flooding in as you become a vibrational match. Open the door and submerge yourself in the messiness of your beautiful human self.

Let Your Intuition Flourish

As you heal and remove the layers and blocks that have kept you stagnant, you will also start to notice your intuition flourish as you embrace the new you! Now that you've reconnected to yourself, you'll notice that your intuition will be heightened and you'll be sensing more.

Many people ask me how they can become intuitive; the great news is we're all born with this ability, but we just need to activate and develop it like any skill.

The inner work can often "block" your third eye (your intuition) – you may have felt like you got the wrong guidance in the past or didn't get anything at all come through. There are many things that can block this connection, so clearing the blocks and layers of resistance through inner work will allow you to be a clear channel and develop this skill.

Listening is key with your intuition so take the time to trust those nudges or niggles that come up, and use divination tools such as oracle cards, tarot or crystals to help you practise this.

Listening to your intuition and honouring this will also help the beautiful journey of discovering the new you. Let your intuition guide you to what's next and what you should explore!

Now let's put that intuition to the test and help you discover some breadcrumbs along the path to meeting the new you. This a meditation that I've done with my coaching clients for a few years now and I love it! Not only does it help you to get clear on the next steps but it also allows you to tune in to your higher self for guidance.

"What Shall I do Next?" Meditation

1. Close your eyes and make sure you're sitting comfortably.

2. Now think about your career, direction, or whatever you'd like clarity on in your mind. With your eyes closed, see a beautiful, white-golden light come down from a few centimetres (or inches) above your head (the point of your crown chakra). See this white-golden light pour into your head and all the way down through your body, illuminating you until it reaches your toes.

3. Bring this white-golden light back up into your heart centre in the middle of your chest and allow it to sit there.

4. I now want you to see yourself sitting in the space that you're in (with your eyes still closed) and see yourself five years in the future. Take note of what this version of yourself is doing. What is this self doing day to day? What are they wearing? Where are they? Keep a mental note of all the details you pick up on and finally ask them, "What advice do you have for me here and now?" and listen for a response.

5. Next, fast forward to ten years in the future and again take note of what's happening now for your future self. What is this version of you doing? What are they doing day to day? How are they feeling? Where are they? Keep a mental note of all the details you see around you and finally ask them, "What advice do you have for me here and now?" and listen for a response.

6. Thank both the five- and ten-year future versions of yourself for their advice and wisdom.

7. Next, come back to your self five years from now, and finally back into your body here and now. Take a deep breath in and let it go.

8. Write down what you saw in both the five years' time and ten years from now meditations, noting down how these selves were feeling and what advice they had for you. Use this advice moving forward and think about how you can take action toward reaching what the five years from now version of you was doing. How can you embody this here and now?

Set an intention with the Universe today to be shown through signs, synchronicities and people how to meet the new you and discover this new Healed identity through fun, joy and new opportunities. Life is a discovery of self and this is a new exciting chapter – one in which you get to fully know yourself, be yourself and express yourself unconditionally.

⁺✦ **PRACTICE** ✦⁺

Journaling prompts
- "What do I need today?"
- "How can I show up authentically today?"
- "How can I inspire others to be their true self today?"
- "What would the best version of me do today?"

Intention
Complete the "What Shall I Do Next?" meditation on page 147. Set an intention with the Universe today to help you through signs, synchronicities and people to meet the new you and to discover this new Healed identity through fun, joy and new opportunities.

Activity
Write your appreciation list – a list of all the moments you've overcome and grown from. These could also be moments you're really proud of. Write down as many points as you can. You can always add to this list in the future as you remember more things or overcome something new. Keep this list safe or you could proudly display it somewhere in your home so you can remind yourself of these points regularly.

Action
Finally, what can you do today to celebrate your appreciation list and yourself – because you're bloomin' marvellous! How can you celebrate your uniqueness and beauty? Throw yourself a dance party, treat yourself with your friends, play with your inner child. Whatever it is, give yourself permission to fully be you today, authentically, beautifully, messy you – and celebrate!

Creating the Space and Balance

Balance is something I have been challenged to create at numerous points in my life, whether it's a work–life balance or finding balance emotionally or spiritually. Balance has definitely been a big lesson for me with manifesting and creating fulfilment within myself too. Although I thought I had great balance in my life, it was only when I was forced to create balance when my health came to the forefront that I was shocked to find I had a long way to go!

Being naturally more in my divine masculine energy means that I have a very get-up-and-go, motivated attitude, which, mixed with my Virgo sun sign, gives you an indication of how hardworking I am and how I've got to where I am today through hard work, dedication and consistency.

When my relationships were difficult and it felt like that area was out of my control, I dived into work. It was the one thing I could control and the one thing that brought me happiness in those dark times.

I mentioned in Chapter 1 how, as I worked through the Healing stage of my journey, my physical body developed a hormone imbalance and I suffered with cystic acne for a few years. No matter what I did it didn't budge, so I turned to holistic help and worked on balancing my divine feminine energy. But even after embracing my beautiful feminine energy, womb space, cycles and healing the spiritual and cognitive side to my inner work – still the acne wouldn't shift.

Now, when I say I tried every supplement and healing modality under the sun, I really did, and my loved ones were just as baffled as me. I even paid privately for a specialist and had every hormone, fertility and adrenal test going – which all come back as normal and healthy. Which once again left me baffled! It took a lot of self-love, self-acceptance and patience with this journey.

In 2020, I had a psychic reading with my friend and client Trish, who said, "You need to create balance for this relationship you want to come in." At the time I couldn't understand where I could create any more balance and space in my life, until my health stopped me right in my tracks. At that moment I realized I needed help, as I had been running my businesses as a one-man band for eight years and, as I described earlier, I was exhausted.

So I made big moves and hired a lovely operations manager who I ended up manifesting as she'd already been my PR manager. Taking on Donna lifted a heavy weight I'd been carrying, and slowly it became so easy to hand over multiple areas of my business and daily tasks to help me find balance – and it was the best move I've ever made.

Next came sorting out my house. Even though I'm super tidy, there were things I needed to get around to and that needed clearing or upgrading, so once again I allowed myself to be supported by family and loved ones by asking for their help with this.

Slowly but surely, I found my energy returning, I made big energy shifts and put in boundaries at work which once again helped me to create the space and find that all important balance. As I found balance, I realized my skin was also getting better with the help of Vitamin E and antibiotics (to clear the infection). I felt better within myself and this even spurred me on to lose 6.5kg (1½ stone) of weight I'd put on by being too busy and not looking after my health.

So as I found this balance in my life, everything else started to balance out and I realized that my body has been under extreme amounts of stress over the years due to work and my previous relationships – in fact, it was a bloomin' miracle that cystic acne was the *only* thing wrong with me!

As I reflected on all the shifts, abundance and happiness I felt from finding this divine balance in my life, I realized exactly what Trish had said in my reading five months prior. There was no way I could have sustained a relationship and given myself fully to someone when I wasn't even doing that for myself! Now, with this balance in place, I knew I could welcome in that special relationship, focus on my personal life and let my work-life balance support me even as I stepped back to create the space.

When Less is More

A great mantra I worked with over this time was "Emma does less, Emma attracts more". At first this was a joke between me and my friends about earning more money by doing less hard grafting day to day. Then I realized how much magic was in this mantra and how it held the secret to everything for me. Over this time, not only did my mantra bring divine balance into my life, it created the space for my biggest desires to manifest finally and allowed me to fully receive from the Universe.

We all need to incorporate this kind of energy into our manifesting practice. We can be so eager to go all in and do everything in our power to make things happen, that we forget we need to create the space and move into the important stage of letting go and surrendering in order to start manifesting.

When we're healing our energetic space is full because we're focusing on clearing and releasing the past. Compare it to a house: if you want to buy a new lamp but your living room is already full, you're not going to have anywhere nice to display this new lamp. So you create the space by selling or getting rid of what you already have. The same works with manifesting: you need to create the space for your desire to come in.

So my earlier example – about getting the support I needed – was about creating balance so that I had the time and emotional space to be committed to the relationship when it manifested. There was not enough space before, because my work was filling it!

In the same way, challenge yourself now as you move past the Healing stage into Healed to look at your physical home and work space, and to look at your time or schedule or even where you invest yourself emotionally. Where do you need to create the space?

The easiest way to create balance and space in your life is by embracing simplicity. We all know how fashionable the minimalist life and home are now, but actually there's some great wisdom behind this! Now, I'm not telling you to empty your house and live a minimalistic lifestyle, but how can you simplify your life? How can you take things back to basics to create the space?

My friend Kaitlyn and I made a big discovery when we were feeling frustrated that our biggest desires still weren't here, no matter what we did. We wanted to rebel and give up as we'd done the inner work (we really had completed countless hours of working with mentors) and we'd been showing up for the Universe through our work too; it made no sense.

So one day Kaitlyn messaged me and said, "Emma, I sat down earlier and realized that every single time I've manifested something big in my life I've been doing absolutely nothing!" This statement shocked me so I thought, "Okay, let's see about mine?" and low and behold I looked at all my biggest manifestations and guess what? I too was doing nothing at the time! What I mean by nothing, is no inner work – we were just living our lives and allowing things to manifest without forcing anything.

This got me thinking even deeper into why this had worked for us, and I said, "Kaitlyn, we need a no fucks given attitude! Think about it, did you give any fucks at the time or were you deeply surrendered?" We both agreed we were deeply surrendered and didn't care as we were just busy "being".

This hit me hard as Kaitlyn and I are both Virgo sun signs, meaning "just being" is a practice that doesn't come easily to us. We were usually so busy trying to "fix" ourselves or achieve more that we forgot to just be. So we committed in that moment to doing no more, as we knew we had done the inner work, and to just being and not giving a fuck.

At first this felt rebellious; we were going against all old Law of Attraction teachings that said "If your desire isn't here then you have more work to do; there's something wrong", and once again I was reminded how less really is more sometimes with manifesting. There is a time and place for the inner work as we know, but there is also a time and place for joy, fun and living your life!

Within a few weeks, Kaitlyn and I both saw big manifestations come into our lives – not the ones we were letting go of, but others we equally had wanted for a while. Kaitlyn made big, bold moves to create space in her life, while I listened to my heart and stopped doing so much (which most people might think would be counterproductive toward my manifestation), because it didn't feel good anymore. We listened to ourselves fully – no one else; we created simplicity and we allowed ourselves to just be. We didn't chase, we let ourselves receive fully.

There is magic in this process and it's really important to do this authentically at the stage where you are past the inner work. (You can't force yourself to do this step, you definitely have to lean into it.) Creating simplicity is a life-changing practice that invites in balance and the very space needed to manifest your desires.

Remember, less is more with manifesting and I really do fully believe this, having seen it work in my life numerous times as I adopted my "Emma does less, Emma attracts more" mantra. So often people come to me having tried every manifestation practice going – even hearing them tell me what they do on a daily basis feels overwhelming. We don't need to be doing all the time and we certainly don't need to be overdoing it with manifestation. Simplicity is key – so keep it simple and remember to keep your practices fun. You want to be able to maintain and keep up with your practices even when your desires are here so you have the time and space to enjoy them.

I want you to commit to creating space and balance in your life now. You've done the work and it's time to embrace all that is and live life, because there is so much beauty and power in the now. Living is also a great manifestation tool! When you create simplicity and feel gratitude in the now, you create a powerful container for shifts, abundance and fulfilment.

Allow Yourself to Receive

Next, I want to talk about the power of receiving because again this is something we don't often do as empaths and spiritual folk. Being selfless is a great quality to have, of course, but as I described earlier, we have to allow ourselves to receive too. We have to allow the Universe to meet us halfway and deliver.

I had a few blocks around receiving with my inner child and in relationships due to past hurt and experiences. Allowing myself to be held felt like a big, scary move to make as I have always had to support myself in so many ways. But if I didn't allow myself to receive in all areas of my life, how could I expect to be held by the masculine in love? How could I expect the Universe to deliver my desires if I wasn't leaning in to that receiving stage?

Hopefully by now you're leaning in to the receiving stage more naturally and allowing yourself to be held, supported and receive in all areas of your life. If you feel like you may still have some resistance around this then go back to the previous chapters to support you with uncovering this inner work. Put down the mountains you've been carrying because you don't have to do this alone. By slowing down, taking a step back and allowing, you are truly letting yourself receive from the Universe instead of standing in your own way and blocking abundance. By stepping back and stepping down from what's no longer serving you or cluttering your life, you allow yourself to step up into this new chapter of abundance.

Make a Big Queen Move

Another major way to create the space if you feel you've done the above and shifts still aren't happening, is to look at what big Queen moves you can make.

I'm always reluctant to suggest this as only you yourself can make the decision about whether this is right for you. I once had a client who had again done the inner work so well – she was creating the space and feeling great. Then one session she came back and explained how restricted she still felt by her current role at work and although it paid well, it wasn't bringing her joy anymore. My intuition said, "Tell her to quit", but of course I wanted to dive deeper before making a big suggestion like this. Luckily, though, my client could support herself financially and her partner had also suggested she leave her job countless times, so there were no worries there: the Universe was supporting her fully. I asked her how she'd feel in a month's time if she left the job and she said, "Fucking amazing!" I actually wasn't expecting such a clear answer from her!

It seemed like a no-brainer: if she wanted her dream job and career, she had done everything else except make a big leap of faith. This won't be the case for everyone. For example, I worked part-time in a clothes shop while I set up my first business to pay off my debts and support myself, and even when setting up my current business I still ran my previous couponing business for a year in the background to financially support myself. So this really will come down to your own circumstances and free will to make your choice.

For my client, she knew deep down what to do, so I was just helping her come to that decision by offering more points of view. A few days after our session, my client emailed me and said that the very same day she decided to hand in her notice, her agent contacted her and said she had got a confirmed role in her dream career! She couldn't believe how quickly this had happened and how making a big Queen move like this had allowed her to receive what she *did* want.

Remember, big leaps of faith bring big rewards even if they may seem counter-intuitive at the time. For my client, her current role was in her chosen area of expertise, but it wasn't what she truly wanted to be doing. So many would have said that doing that role would have continued to help her, but she knew deep down if it wasn't feeling good anymore it had to go!

With that brave move she opened up the door to abundance and alignment too. I have had this happen countless times with my own manifestations – the key is to really listen to your intuition and take those leaps when you feel called to. Sometimes we have to be brave enough to let go of the old or the familiar in order to create the space for new energy and abundance to enter. Big leaps bring big rewards so, Queen, don't be afraid to take that leap if you know that's what is holding you back and cluttering your energetic space.

The power of decluttering in all areas of your life is powerful, whether it's energetically, physically or emotionally; maybe it's about changing one small habit, letting in support or trying something new. Today, I want you to really sit with this chapter and adopt the mantra for yourself: "(Name) does less, (Name) attracts more."

Now that you have the energetic space to receive after the Healing stage, it's time to clear away the cobwebs in your life, spring clean your life in all areas and create the space for your biggest desires to come in through decluttering and simplifying your life and manifestations. Less is more so – challenge yourself to think about your manifesting process currently and what needs a good declutter and revamp with this new energy.

⁺⁺ ✦ PRACTICE ✦ ⁺⁺

Journaling prompts
- "What areas do I need to create balance in?"
- "How can I create space in my life, home or work space?"
- "How can I simplify my life and manifesting process?"
- "How can I allow myself to receive more in everyday life?"

Intention
Adopt my mantra of "Emma does less, Emma attracts more" using your own name and work with this mantra's energy by repeating this once a day over the next 21 days either through journaling or saying it to yourself in the mirror. Commit to embracing simplicity in your manifesting process and declutter anything from your spiritual or manifesting practices that need shifting or new energy.

Activity
Using your answers to the journaling prompts, take action and declutter your life as necessary. Create the space in your mind, home or work space to shift the energy. You could also make a list of how you can simplify your life whether this is with your daily to-do list /chores or areas of your life that are feeling stressful currently.

Action
Commit to not giving a fuck now and allowing yourself to truly receive. Allow yourself to fully be present and enjoy life here and now. Listen to your heart and stop doing anything that doesn't feel good to you and make the time and space for things that do feel good and light up your soul. Honour yourself and make those big brave moves if it feels good to.

Maintaining Momentum

Now that you're steadily working through the Healed phase, it's important to focus on how you can maintain this positive momentum, energy and healing, moving forward. The secret to balance and consistency is found in your daily routine and having a practice that works for you. Whether you call this a spiritual routine or simply a routine that helps you raise your vibes and feel good, all that matters is that it feels good to you and is fun!

As you work through the layers of your spiritual journey, hurdles or healing may arise. As I've mentioned earlier, you will go through seasons of outer, masculine, manifesting and summer energy when you feel very outward-facing, and then periods of inner, winter, feminine hibernation energy when some healing may arise. Just like yin and yang energy, without one we wouldn't be able to appreciate the other.

Things may come up in life and knock you down or challenge you to up-level but now you have the tools and awareness to deal with anything that arises. If you've been working on a particular wound or belief during this book, a new layer to this may arise in the future – it's important to witness any new layers with grace and gentleness. The inner work will always be there, but it's important that you're living your life and having fun too.

Balance the Inner Work with Play

Over the years, I've seen many people become obsessed with inner work and the drive to be constantly doing it. This is great if it's something that genuinely needs to be worked on – but when do you stop? When is enough, enough?

This is why you have to use your discernment and know when you need inner and outer periods of rest and play. Doing the inner work constantly will bore you and your inner child eventually, no matter how much fun it may be at first. Continuously looking at your traumas, limiting beliefs and every thought and behaviour can be very draining. Not everything needs to be worked on and I feel I need to say that to the avid inner workers out there and even remind myself of this sometimes. So make sure to take regular time out and focus on having fun and making memories too. Earth may be our classroom but we're here to experience all the things this world has to offer, not just healing and inner work.

You will make mistakes, you will get things wrong, you will feel triggered at points and you may or may not have new things come up. But it's all about how you handle it and navigate the journey. Not everything is a sign you need to do inner work; I always suggest sitting with the feelings or emotions before I jump to book in a session with one of my coaches or therapists. Very often the new or full moon, solstice or equinoxes or even planetary changes can all affect our moods, energy and emotions, as I shared earlier in Chapter 11. So it's important to sit with your feelings and emotions to really tune in and see what is underneath them. Is it something that can be fixed by your daily practice and a nice walk in nature to clear your head? Is it something that sharing with your friends and loved one could help? Would some yoga or dance help shift the energy through you? Maybe your body is even calling for you to sleep and rest?

Whatever it is, it's important we honour our bodies and feelings. In the depths of my healing seasons, I've slept for hours each day. At those times, I've had to drop my judgement over productivity and remember my body is healing and releasing a lot, so rest is actually productive in order for my body to recover.

This is why it's important to make your daily practice intuitive and honour what you and your energy need that day. Sometimes you'll have more energy and want to be out and about doing things, and other days you may want to hibernate in bed and your daily practice may be slower and more restful. Whatever brings you the most joy and energy is always the right answer and it's important to mix up your rituals regularly to keep the spark of joy there.

Taking care of yourself and your energy is a form of self-love, so you can see that your daily practice is about more than just raising your vibes; it's about weaving in all you've learned throughout this book on self-care, self-love, balance and energy to maintain this positive momentum moving forward.

Make Your Daily Practice Work for You

I've mentioned earlier how inner work is like working through the layers of an onion, and as we work through the layers, these become smaller and smaller. So each time it will feel less intense as you move through the layer more quickly and release it.

Having a solid daily practice in place will allow you to navigate these layers with ease and grace on stormier days, and help you feel aligned and uplifted on calmer days. Think of it like a skincare routine you do each day to make sure your face is clean and prepped for the day ahead – your spiritual practice works the same way. We've spoken about the importance of gratitude and how to incorporate this into your day, but let's take it a bit deeper now.

As we discussed in Chapter 2 when you first started cultivating your daily routine, it doesn't need to feel like a burden or take up lots of time, nor do you have to wake up super early. The key is to keep it feeling fun and energizing.

Many of my clients struggle to juggle this with having babies or young children they need to see to in the morning – so if this is you, make your routine work around your schedule. As long as you're doing it as close to waking up as possible that's all that matters.

It may even be worth setting your alarm for 10 to 15 minutes earlier each morning to create the space for this. Your daily gratitude practice should take you around 5 minutes to complete, but now comes the fun part as you get to create the rest! Whether that means something like yoga or stretching, breathwork, EFT, affirmations, mirror work, journaling, meditation or anything else you enjoy doing, your daily practice is *your* daily practice and it's all about adding in practices and exercises that feel fun to you and raise your vibration.

The Benefits of Your Daily Routine

There are so many amazing benefits to having a daily practice. The experiences of many people show the health benefits, such as a reduced risk of breast cancer, reduced stress and the decreased risk of developing anxiety and depression, and even illnesses like high blood pressure, heart disease and diabetes. As a daily routine can considerably lower stress, this helps raise your vibration – which means you're in a fantastic energy to receive abundance.

If that wasn't enough, a survey conducted in December 2021 by The Sleep Judge found that respondents who stuck to a strict morning routine earned a whopping $12,500 (roughly £10,000) more per year than those who described a more casual approach to the morning.

Some other fantastic benefits are that it prepares you for the rest of the day and allows you to feel organized and calm in the morning. It increases your productivity and means you spend time on something valuable, which sets you up for success in the rest of your day. You feel in control and can handle anything that disrupts your day in a calmer and more positive way.

Waking up earlier and carving out the time to do your morning ritual in a relaxed fashion will boost your energy levels and those positive vibes. You develop healthy habits that stay with you throughout the day and may mean you want to eat more healthily, exercise before you go to work or even just be more mindful and spend less time on your phone.

Having a structured morning routine will also help improve your relationships, including your relationship with yourself as you'll be less likely to take any stresses out on your loved ones and feel calmer and happier within yourself by dedicating time to a self-loving practice like this. It will also improve your confidence as you go throughout your day, helping you to combat forgetfulness as you have more time to gather yourself in the morning, and it will help you to be flexible and deal with any disruptions that may happen throughout your day from a calmer and more aligned place. So, if these aren't AMAZING reasons to create and stick to a morning routine I don't know what are!

So take the time today to think about what exercises and practices you've really enjoyed in this book and what you feel could be included in a positive daily routine that will help to raise your vibes. Remember that your daily routine only needs to take up 10 to 15 minutes out of your day and can be completed in the morning or parts of it can scattered throughout your day, depending on your schedule. I would strongly suggest doing your gratitude practice as soon as you wake up, and then anything else can be done at the same time or throughout your day when you have the time and energy for it.

Ending Your Day Well

Another point to note is that if you're doing evening practices or using any of the above suggestions before you go to bed to wind down, make sure they are not too mentally stimulating.

Online frequency (healing) meditations, for example, are great, but a lot of my clients have reported not being able to sleep properly while they've been listening to them as it's too stimulating for their minds late at night.

EFT is another practice best done in the morning or during the daytime as it activates and shifts your energetic centres (meridian points), meaning that it gives you a burst of energy.

Meditation can be great to relax to and many people choose to fall asleep to meditation, which helps them switch off for the day. However, the meditations mentioned in this book are activating and require your input so I would suggest doing them in the daytime for full effect.

Sometimes placing really active crystals next to your bed can also disrupt your sleep patterns and dreams, so all of these things are worth considering if your sleep pattern has been disrupted or if you plan to do some of these rituals at night time.

Look at your sleep hygiene and see if there is any room for improvement. Maybe it means switching your phone off earlier and having some you time before you go to sleep? Maybe it's writing down a bedtime routine to ensure you do your skincare routine and spiritual practices if you tend to forget these? Setting yourself up for sleep success is really important so that you feel rested and energized for the next day.

As much as your daily practice can set you up for success, so can your night-time practice. I'm much more relaxed when it comes to night-time routines. While it's important to do them just like brushing your teeth and your skincare routine, I'm much more intuitive with mine. I don't force myself to do anything; I go with the flow and see what my energy can do at that time of night. Sometimes I can only do my gratitude practice and I'm asleep, other nights I'll do more and even incorporate my self-care steps for the week into this. When you can see how daily habits and routines like this are just as important as your skincare routine, you'll never want to miss them again!

Respect Your Routine

When I fall out of my routine and don't prioritize my rituals and practices, my mood and energy can slip. Especially if work and life are being challenging, and I fall into bad habits, I notice I can feel down, unmotivated and stuck energy-wise. Yet as soon as I take action and do some spiritual practices and up my self-care away from my phone, my mood and energy instantly improve.

So please use this as your reminder each week to take time away from technology and prioritize yourself. As much as this absolutely comes into self-love, maintaining rituals and daily habits that cultivate joy and happiness is vital for any Spiritual Queen in the Healed phase. Life will come and test you and you may face stormy seas from time to time but with the power of your daily habits and rituals you can create momentum, change, abundance and so much more goodness in your life – and quickly.

They say that how you spend the first 20-minutes of your morning shapes your experiences and mood for the day. While I fully agree with this, I want to take it further and share with you that also setting up your week for success is a great way to boost your mood and productivity too. Every Sunday I plan my week ahead and look at what free time I have to do some fun projects and my self-care routine. This allows me to plan my week, meals, wake-up times, breaks and social time. By doing this I make sure each morning that I have enough time to achieve all I need to, so that I'm entering into my day with ease instead of chasing my tail and rushing from one meeting to the next. This then allows me the time to do my daily rituals and carve out time for any other practices that I want to support myself with each day.

Getting yourself into a good routine is key. Just like with a consistent skincare routine you'll see improvements to your skin, the same goes with your daily habits: the more you put in the more you get out.

Only recently I remembered I hadn't done a new moon ritual for a few months as I had let this slip. So I did one there and then as it was the new moon, and instantly, by setting intentions on how I wanted to feel, I felt shifted and optimistic for the month ahead. I immediately started seeing and feeling my intentions, reminding me that by not letting life distract me this simple exercise that only takes me three to five minutes once a month can supercharge my manifestations and help me feel happy and aligned too.

So use this chapter as your permission slip to keep the positive momentum in your life. Or if you feel like your daily habits have slipped recently, use this as a gentle reminder to take some action through the tasks below to invite joy and positive energy back into your life.

⁺⁺ PRACTICE ⁺⁺

Journaling prompts
- "What practices or rituals bring me joy and happiness?"
- "What could I do each day or week to set myself up for success with my daily practice?"

Intention
Set an intention of how you'd like to feel each day in your daily practice. Do this at the end of your gratitude practice or after you've completed each activity. Write down: "Today, I would like to experience ..." And fill in the gap. Then write: "Today, I would like to feel ..." And finally: "Today, I would like to manifest ..." Fill in your answers to these each day and make sure to check back in when you go to bed in the evening to see what manifested throughout your day!

Activity
Get organized and set yourself up for success! Plan your week ahead on a Sunday if possible and carve out time for your morning and evening practice as well as time to fill your own cup and complete your self-care routine. Schedule out time to connect with yourself away from technology and focus on fun projects or rituals to boost your mood.

Action
Create your daily routine or habits as explained in this chapter – what would feel good to include in your morning and evening practice? Mix this up every now and again when it feels right to, or if these activities feel repetitive, but make sure you're doing a gratitude practice each and every day if you can.

My Daily AM Practice	
My Daily PM practice	
My Weekly Self-care Routine	
My Top Priorities This Week	

My Weekly Practices

Aligned Manifesting and Abundance

A few years ago, I thought I'd manifested my dream life. I had manifested everything from my original vision board and was like, "Woah, I did it!" Yet something didn't feel right. No matter how much I manifested I still felt sadness and anxiety under the surface. To the world, I had manifested my dreams but underneath it was a very different reality.

This part of my journey inspired me to go along my *Positively Wealthy* journey and write my second book to redefine my version of wealth, find true fulfilment within myself and sustainably manifest abundance.

So why didn't my dream life feel right? Because I wasn't in true alignment. I had inner work to do and the Universe was taking me on that journey through these experiences and karmic events. Manifesting it all showed me how *my* version of abundance wasn't really what I truly wanted and that I still had some healing to do in order to realize and take action to manifest my true aligned vision of happiness with the Universe.

Many people who are interested in the Law of Attraction don't realize the sort of ground work that also needs to go into manifesting your dream life – the real inner work of alignment, harmony and peace that are required to manifest that dream life in your outer experience. Some aren't prepared to put in the work because of fear or lack of interest; but as someone who did put in the work, I found myself questioning my faith and everything I believed in when I sat there surrounded by a dream life that felt so wrong.

So where did it go wrong? I don't think there was one particular reason why, nor do I believe it was "wrong" as such. I believe it was destiny that I had to go along this journey to show me there was a better way if I only learned to let go and allow the Universe to show me I deserved more. I was settling for way less and I needed to fully embody my healing and allow my vibration to match this new version of myself to call in the aligned abundance that was waiting for me on the next level.

This is something I see too often in the online sphere and hear from people too. They reach the top of their career, they earn the life-changing money, they manifest all their desires – yet their best life isn't actually that peaceful and when I say peaceful, I mean that you know when something is for you by the way it feels.

Back then, when all the things I'd ever wanted lined up, I felt anxious, I felt triggered and then, when things became stressful, that's when my body started to physically react too. I remember reading a quote that said, "You'll know it's meant for you by the way it feels and how your nervous system responds", and now that I am in a totally different space of my life – healed, happy and aligned – my body fully agrees with this. Before I didn't feel safe and my nervous system knew that. It was telling me something was wrong but at first I ignored my body, the stress, the signs, the red flags – all of it. I also went through a phase where I stopped manifesting for a while and my life felt stuck.

I know I'm not alone in this and I feel this happens to so many people because we think we know what's meant for us, we believe we know what is for our highest good and then we learn why something we really wanted isn't sustainable or for our highest good; or we settle for realities out of fear and convenience rather than what truly feels good to us.

Now, that's not to say we don't need those experiences – of course we do, to teach us and show us what does feel good and what we want, moving forward – but too many of us wait until our manifestation falls away until we realize that it wasn't in alignment with us and the Universe in the first place. We wonder why the dream house fell through, why the dream career didn't last or why the dream partner didn't work out.

Months went past that turned into years where I felt like I was stuck in a loop and couldn't understand why I was doing the inner work without seeing the physical results. I do think this comes down to two reasons, one being divine timing, but also when we're in the Healing stage our energy is focused on this inner work – and energy flows where intention goes. Often where you enter into the healing cocoon and the focus is just on you for a while, you experience a more inward winter journey of the divine feminine energy, rather than an outer summer manifesting experience of the divine masculine energy.

Alignment is key, though, and looking back at the last 12 months of my life I'm left feeling blown away. When I finally took back all my energy and dedicated myself to deep inner work and releasing the past, creating divine balance in my life and healing my body, the Universe delivered in big, big ways.

Manifesting from an Aligned Space

My friend and I were recently reflecting on the last year and how 12 months ago we felt stuck and in the inner work trenches so to speak, but now we have both just manifested major things, and the dreams of ours that felt stuck for so long are now here for both of us. I believe the secret to these successes is alignment and manifesting from an aligned space too.

The life I live now feels so different – even polar opposite to what I thought it would look like – but it feels like everything I've wanted and more. The peace I feel is the biggest indication for me of alignment and the safety that also comes with that alignment.

Having hopefully moved through the Healing stage as you enter into this new Healed phase, you're going to be in this aligned space too. Only you can answer whether your current circumstances or desires are aligned, so ask yourself honestly: "Does this allow my body to feel calm and at peace or do I feel anxious or on edge about it?" Feeling is everything with the Law of Attraction and when I spoke about tuning in to the core energy and emotion of your desire in an earlier chapter, this is again an extension of this.

When I tuned in to the relationship I really wanted, it felt safe, it felt so held and peaceful – and the emotions I feel now are exactly that. I could breathe easily and feel at ease, and my body also felt at ease in my partner's energy, which again was a big indicator to me this was an aligned manifestation.

When things are meant for us they can happen quickly and sometimes it can feel like we're not even in control and the Universe is moving us in ways we couldn't see before.

Manifesting from a Grounded Place

On reflection, I realize now that the main reason I felt my dream life wasn't what I thought it would be back then was because it could all have been taken away from me. By this, I mean that if it had been taken away, then my "happiness" would have disappeared with it – which meant my version of abundance, wealth and fulfilment at that time relied on external factors, so was not aligned with inner abundance or peace.

Buddhist teachings often refer to happiness and fulfilment as being an inside job and say that if your happiness is reliant on external factors you'll always be unhappy. That is exactly how I felt and I'm sure you can relate to this at some stage in your life too.

The way we create aligned abundance is through grounding and manifesting stable roots that can't be shaken. It's about getting to a place where you feel whole and complete within yourself – and where everything could be stripped away and you'd still be okay.

That's an uncomfortable thought to sit with, but so important when it comes to aligned manifesting and feeling complete within yourself first. Only you can give yourself that gift; and when I did, my whole life changed forever. Things I'd wanted for years flooded in, surprised me and nourished me like never before.

So this is about manifesting from a peaceful, fulfilled place rather than a fearful one. Which at the beginning of our journey can be hard, because we think that manifesting certain things will lead to a fulfilled place from which we can then manifest the rest. Well, Queen, I hate to say it but that's not true – it never has been and as someone who's lived it, it just doesn't happen. If I'd known this information at the beginning of my journey, my manifesting would have looked completely different.

To manifest from a grounded place, tune in to your heart and in to your inner wisdom, and ask yourself whether your desires are aligned for the highest good of all. How does your body react? Take notes and observe, get still and present and enquire. The Universe makes no mistakes, so while it is saying yes to us, it's really saying yes to alignment and whatever is for the highest good of all – not just *your* version of the desire.

Create Your Own Safe Container of Friends for Manifesting

Another thing to consider when cultivating your manifesting practices, moving forward, is to create safe containers for them. Safe containers are what create beautifully aligned desires – which means that you don't tell just anyone what you're co-creating in your world. Keeping things private for as long as you need to will help the Universe bring all the pieces together and stops any unwanted interference from outside influences that may not be in alignment or which could negatively influence you during this creation process.

Just tell your sacred circle (your soul sisters and soul family who you can deeply trust) and that's it – no one else. You want clean energy going toward your desires.

Then protect and incubate your desires until it feels right to share them with the world. There is no rush and although it's exciting to share amazing news and abundance, it's got to feel aligned to you. You don't owe anyone anything but you owe it to yourself to birth these desires in a safe, held container surrounded by love.

From doing this myself over the years, it's beautiful what unfolds when your soul family/sisters hold that space and all of your desires are protected in that safe container. The aligned abundance I've been able to create today was formed in these beautiful containers with my soul family holding me every step of the way, and with me supporting them as well. They have shared with me how they held visions and intentions for me for the highest good after witnessing everything I'd been through, and I know what I'm living now is an expression of their co-creation and wishes for me too. Together we've manifested relationships, pets, book deals, music success, money and much more!

So aligned abundance can come from your soul family as well. Not only can you hold the space for your friends' desires, it's about holding the most aligned vision for them too and seeing them happy. These containers create magic and are a great way to manifest together.

You could do this in a private group on social media or even on a WhatsApp group. Have your sacred circle include just a few people and make it a group full of gratitude, joy, manifestations and support.

Cultivate a Miracle Mindset

Creating a miracle mindset also encourages aligned manifesting and abundance. Miracles can be as small as a shift in awareness or clarity, to your biggest manifestations coming into fruition. There are no limits to how big or how many miracles you can receive.

Cultivating a miracle mindset means you become a magnet to miracles – and this starts off with seeing opportunities in times of difficulty or discomfort. No matter how hard a situation may be, ask yourself: "What is this giving me the opportunity to do?" When you can find the opportunity in any given moment, you create the capacity for miracles to enter your life.

Setting intentions is another great way to spark a miracle mindset and invite in support and creative solutions from the Universe when you need them. Think back to all the times the Universe stepped in and created miracles both big and small in your life. Miracles flow to us every day – we just have to be in flow with a miracle mindset to see them.

Check Yourself Before You Wreck Yourself

Now let's talk about how you can start to manifest from an aligned space in your life. If you've read my second book *Positively Wealthy*, you'll be familiar with looking at each area of your life and being honest about your fulfilment level in each of them. Having awareness is key and manifesting from a space of peace and the present moment is vital.

So looking after yourself is essential – self-love and self-care all the way, baby! Loving yourself unconditionally, like we spoke about before, is the secret to creating true alignment within yourself, which will allow you to feel calm and grounded when co-creating with the Universe. You want to make sure you're in a place of stable energy to manifest aligned abundance. As I mentioned earlier, you won't always feel like this, so it's important to get present in each moment and not react from past conditioning.

When we go through healing and experience new situations from an aligned space, this doesn't mean our fears suddenly disappear. Sometimes the best things in life are unexpected, we don't see them coming, we don't sense them and the Universe sends us the biggest plot twists in the most magical way. But when this happens our inner child and subconscious may kick in and start to question or doubt things. It's the "shock mode" after the manifestation, as I call it.

This is why some people are unable to sustainably keep their manifestations when they materialize – because they either project unhealed inner work on to the new situation or start to self-sabotage. I know I've done this and it really takes a badass Spiritual Queen to be able to witness and recognize when a true feeling or concern has come up, or if your past conditioning or fears are cropping up instead. If they are cropping up, you have to witness them and take action.

Check yourself before you wreck yourself – truly, we can't mess up what's meant for us, but get still, get present and tune in to the fear or emotion. What is it showing you?

The best way to combat this if it starts happening to you during the manifestation process or when your manifestation arrives is by making sure your cup is full and that you're looking after yourself emotionally and physically. When we love and care for ourselves we're able to make better choices and witness things from that aligned, present state – not from our past wounded self like we did before.

Turn Comparisons into Self-awareness

When you are truly looking after yourself, this is also the perfect opportunity to invite in the inner child, and when you can tune in to what your real version of wealth is and what wealth means to you. (Something I explore in detail in *Positively Wealthy*.) You can then manifest from an aligned space of authenticity and peace, rather than anxiety and a version of yourself that feels they have to manifest something because everyone else is manifesting it – which leads us on to the subject of comparison.

Comparison has been described as the thief of joy but actually we can use our moments of comparison to reflect and ask ourselves why we really want this desire. Then we can determine whether it's in alignment with us and the Universe, or not. Are you manifesting something because you've seen someone else have it and you want it too? Or are you manifesting it because it feels good to your soul and feels like a hell YASS?

A powerful way to reframe comparison is by using it as a manifestation tool. Yes, we may need to see if there is anything beneath this that needs healing first, so please dive into any comparisons and see if you need to revisit Part Two to help release any wounds that it relates to. But if there isn't a limiting belief or fear underneath it, then reframe your lack into an opportunity to celebrate the person that you are comparing yourself with. How can you celebrate their achievements and be happy for them? Once you reframe it in this way, use this powerful mantra that my good friend and spiritual peer Lucy Sheridan shared with me: "Good for you and the same for me."

Dealing with Doubts, Discomfort and Uncertainty

Comparison will happen and it's also normal to sometimes doubt things. Every big plot twist in my life that I've received from the Universe, whether it's been a book deal, a relationship or even the house I live in, all happened out of nowhere, which left me in shock mode, not knowing what the "right" thing was to do. I questioned, I doubted, I wondered whether these were meant for me – but in every situation, I trusted, I flowed and I made the right decisions by allowing things to unfold as they needed too. Even if I tried to resist them, the Universe would keep me on that path; so truly know that no matter how much inner work we do, we're all still winging it.

Confliction is real, doubts happen and somehow we all still navigate life and end up where we're meant to. From speaking to numerous clients, peers and coaches over the years, I've found that the themes are the same. We're never going to have an instruction manual for our biggest dreams – they will be new and feel scary, but that's part of this experience here on this Earth. We can't go into every situation prepared and perfect, we have to learn on the job. We may fuck up, we may get it wrong but that's what makes us human. We have to be vulnerable enough to allow ourselves to fully enjoy life and our manifestations from an aligned space. So really receiving aligned manifestations and abundance takes vulnerability – it takes courage and the art of getting still in the discomfort and navigating life with honesty and openness.

Looking back over my manifesting journey, the biggest things I've manifested have felt the scariest – not before they arrived but when they actually did. They've also looked different to how I imagined they would do, but the Universe has never got it wrong. So give yourself permission to co-create with the Universe in an aligned way, where you release the need to control and keep your focus on alignment rather than outcomes and what you can gain.

A great question to ask yourself when manifesting is: "How can this positively impact the collective as well?" When you can identify your why and how your wishes will positively impact the world too, the whole game changes. Tune in to the core energy and emotion of the desire, and trust that even plot twists can be beautiful redirections to a new destination you never thought possible.

How does your body respond to the desire and how does it make you feel? How can you allow your manifestations to feel good and more in alignment? For some, this may involve big upheaval and an honest look at their vision boards, dream lists and wishes, etc.; while for others it could simply be about releasing attachment or looking at things from a new perspective.

Sometimes we have to step back, then step down (for example, by releasing something that's no longer serving us) to be able to step up and align with our desires and this next level. So this is the perfect time to declutter anything from your life that is no longer serving you. Whether physically, emotionally or spiritually, what can you witness as you step back to step up now?

The Universe will surprise you and that's not a bad thing. The most predictable things haven't been in alignment for me personally and did fall away – but the scary, unexpected plot twists? Well, they take courage and big-ass vulnerability, as the Queen Brené Brown would say, and that's how you know when something is in alignment: by the way it feels and how expansive it feels to you and your life.

Recently, I was reflecting on my own alignment and manifestations and realized I haven't put pen to paper recently when asking. I'd had fleeting thoughts of "oh wouldn't that be nice", but I wasn't taking the time to get clear and set those intentions properly. So I sat down and made some big goals that had felt too scary to write down before in my business – and they felt so good to write down and get clear on. I realized they weren't scary and that actually I needed to put energy toward these by writing them down and being brave and bold enough to ask. Within 20 minutes of doing this, I took action and reached out to some legendary people I'd love to interview on my podcast and one got back to me straight away, saying yes! This is the Universe in action: we must always go first and then the Universe makes its move – and something as simple as taking the time to set regular goals and push ourselves to write down those "big" dreams of ours results in alignment, shifts and abundance.

To me, aligned abundance means, yes, setting intentions and honouring yourself in the moment and your desires. But alignment is a continuous process to tune in to as we grow and evolve along the way. Alignment is experiencing and feeling pleasure in your everyday life. Alignment is about expressing your truth and true self, as we looked at in Chapter 12, but also witnessing when something doesn't feel good. Alignment means you're in the present moment and flowing with life and unconditional love. Alignment feels safe, good and steady. It doesn't stress the nervous system and although we may get triggered or fears may arise, it means looking at these and knowing this is a normal part of the healing process and to make sure we're stopping, reflecting and witnessing, rather than reacting from our past conditioning or fears.

Alignment is your true state, so coming back into alignment and showing flexibility toward the Universe and your desires allows the highest possible outcome to align and manifest for you.

Journaling prompts

- "How does this manifestation make my nervous system feel – calm or anxious and on edge?"
- "How can my desires positively impact the collective?"
- "What does pleasure mean to me?"
- "How can I experience more pleasure in my daily life?"

Intention

Set an intention with the Universe to show you how you can be more in alignment with your higher self and your desires. You could write this down or say it out loud:

Universe, please show me how I can be more aligned with my truth and live in full alignment. Help me to release anything that stops me from being in alignment with my desires and allow me to show up as my aligned, authentic self now. I also invite pleasure into all I do today. Thank you, thank you, thank you, Universe.

Activity

Get into the energy of alignment and receiving by creating your own sacred manifesting circle with a few trusted spiritual pals. If you'd like to connect with likeminded people, feel free to join my "Law of Attraction Support Group" on Facebook, as we're a large community of positive souls all cheerleading one another, so you can find some new people to manifest with. Start your own group where you share your manifestations, gratitude and positivity, support one another and create a sacred container for all of your desires to come into fruition.

Action

Revisit your vision boards, manifestation box (this can be a shoebox or some sort of container that you decorate and personalize – which includes your desires and manifesting practices), dream lists, etc. and check in with them. How do they make you feel? Do these all still feel in alignment with your true version of wealth and fulfilment? Think about how you can invite the Universe in to co-create these with you and help these feel in alignment.

Preparing for Your Manifestations

Since discovering the Law of Attraction all those years ago, it's safe to say I have studied it in depth and experimented with a lot of tools and modalities along my manifesting journey. But it's still worth remembering we don't know everything and we're not supposed to have it all figured out just yet. I was reminded of this in a coaching session I had with one of my lovely clients, Holly.

Holly and I had been working together for some time and I was blown away by her commitment to growth and healing, and how she took my advice on board each and every time. In one of our sessions, Holly told me she still felt resistance to one of her biggest desires despite us doing inner work and her seeing big shifts in her life already. She asked me to tune in and see where this was coming from. I always do this with clients but when my clients see how intuitive I can get with our sessions, they sometimes ask me anyway if they're not sure.

When I was listening to Holly and trying to locate these recent negative thoughts and inner critic talk, in all honesty I got nothing. I said, "Holly, you realize this is on the cusp now and you're not in the same place as before? I hope you can sense as well how close this dream is to happening – what is the real fear here?" Holly knew herself that her desire was on the cusp – even her acting teacher had told her this. So I dug deeper to help her and what started coming through gave me an awakening into my own manifestations and why we need to prepare for our manifestations.

I asked Holly, "How safe does it feel to receive this desire on a scale of one to ten?" (With one being not safe and ten feeling fully safe). Holly responded with a nine, which confirmed my hunch and musings.

Now, if you still have inner work to do, this next insight won't apply to you just yet; this is for the people who have been doing the inner work and healing journey on a wound or dream for a while. The truth is when you work on a "bigger" manifestation for some time and there's been big resistance, limiting beliefs, fears or even trauma around this desire, it's safe to say it's going to have taken up a lot of your time, energy and focus. We all do this with our ultimate dream or something we've wanted and craved for a long time. Holly and I, for example, had both done the work, oh boy we had: we had shown up, faced it all and had come along in leaps and bounds.

See, when we've invested a lot of time, love, energy, healing and focus into something, it becomes a big focal point for us, and rightly so, but when does enough become enough? When do we then switch into receiving mode?

I realized that I too wasn't doing this with one of my desires, which meant both Holly and I were actually stuck in my third Law of Attraction step, Trust. We were still trying to take inspired action and not fully progressing to step four, Letting Go. This is why Holly couldn't truly feel peace with the present moment – because she still believed there was something wrong with her and her ego, inner child or inner critic was creating these stories to convince her she wasn't ready, which in fact she really was!

When I asked her what lay in the 10 per cent she didn't feel safe about, she explained, "It feels scary because it would change my life forever." Fear of change was really surfacing here for her and for me too.

After some exploring, we uncovered that actually not much would change at all for her and she really could handle the schedule and location changes her dream acting role would require. I then explained how Holly needed to shift her mindset into receiving mode – and I want to share this with you too because it changed the way I manifest forever.

Switch From Action To Receiving

I had switched before from action to receiving, but very unconsciously, so now I'd like this to become a conscious act for both you and me. When we've done deep inner work and healing, we can sometimes think that every single negative thought needs fixing. Wrong, we are human and, as we've seen, we have thousands of thoughts a day. Do all of them manifest? No, I guarantee they don't, but our ego, inner child and inner critic love to find ways to keep us safe.

Holly really didn't have inner work to do at all; it was more to do with her resisting the very change she knew needed to happen to welcome in this desire of hers. The truth is we're going to have negative thoughts sometimes and we need to stop believing that we have to be 100 per cent healed and perfect to receive our manifestations and dreams. I am certainly guilty of believing this one too (it's the inner perfectionism talking again), but we sometimes have to learn on the job. There will be blessings and lessons when your desire comes, this is all part of life and your evolution. And you may have final layers of healing or releasing to do even once your manifestation arrives, which is normal and happens to all of us. So it's important to witness when you actually have inner work to do versus resisting the inevitable change you can sense coming with your desire.

When you're stuck in step three, Trust, you're not progressing forward. So if you know you've done the work and met the Universe halfway – it feels safe to receive your desire and you can sense it's on the cusp of happening – it's time to switch your mindset into step four, Letting Go.

You will have picked up some handy tips in Chapter 9 on this, but I want to focus more now on acting the part and how preparing for your manifestation shows the Universe that you're ready. We have to stop pushing, we have to stop doing at some point, to allow the manifestation and receive our desire. This can be difficult to do if you're an ex-controller like me or if you struggle to stop and allow, and this is where Holly and I were both going wrong.

We were continually trying to fix things or do things to prove we weren't ready when actually this was the ego, inner child or inner critic running the show and not us. So now I asked Holly, "If your desire was to happen tomorrow, would you be prepared? What would you need to have prepared to be able to step into that role?" Holly listed off a few things she could do that related to her diet, lifestyle and appearance for this acting role and I said, "Great! Work on these over the next few weeks."

It was also amazing to hear that, with just these pointers, Holly already felt those negative thoughts and beliefs of hers disappearing, which confirmed what I'd sensed at the beginning of our session.

Prepare to Receive

At this point in my session with Holly, I was even making a mental note of all the things I could do to prepare for my desire too. I was normally so good at doing this unintentionally but somehow I didn't think I could apply it to ALL of my manifestations. (Hey, even I need reminders every now and again!) So after the session, I grabbed my notebook and made a list of all the things I could do to be ready and prepared for my desire to come.

As I've mentioned, I've done this countless times before where I've bought things for manifestations before they were confirmed. For example, before my puppy Luna's dachshund mum was even pregnant, I bought books on how to train my puppy, blankets, a personalized toy with her name on and a few extra little things to get me excited. As always, my parents in particular thought I was mad, but I just *knew*. When I know, I know, and I didn't doubt it this time either, because I knew it was on the cusp and could sense her coming – and guess what? These desires always come in because I'm preparing to receive. I stop pushing and allow the Universe to meet me with my desire.

Now, you only want to buy things if this feels good, aligned and is not going to put you in financial jeopardy if things don't work out. All of the things I bought when I got Luna would keep and would work out even if variables changed in my desire. So take action today, Queen – not inspired action but step into the place of receiving and prepare for your manifestation to come in!

Think about it: when you have a baby you have nine months to prepare for their arrival. You don't just turn up on the day you go into labour and say, "Right, we better get a cot, decorate the nursery and get some baby clothes." No, you prepare to receive your baby in the lead up to their birth. Same thing here, Queen; you don't want to be panicking about getting in shape, having the time in your schedule or the space in your home, for example, *when* it happens. Do yourself a favour and prepare for your desire now. Think about how relaxed you'll feel being prepared and ready to receive your desire at the right moment.

This works every time because we are effectively "acting as if", which is a big part of the Law of Attraction journey. So whether it's decluttering the house and clearing some drawers to welcome in that relationship you desire, whitening your teeth for that acting job, or eating more healthily to feel good within yourself for the holiday you're manifesting or to look great in your wedding dress, whatever it is, prepare yourself to receive and get excited.

Like I've said, this advice only works when you are truly in the step four, the Letting Go stage, and have already taken your inspired action toward your desire. This was not about Holly applying for acting roles, auditioning and training as she had done all of that. She knew her dream role was on the cusp and it was the in-between "waiting" time and the imminent change she could sense that were stirring up these thoughts.

Change can be an exciting phase as you sense the next phase of your life coming in. But we can also resist this, as "big" manifestations can take up a lot of our time and energy, so it can feel scary to release this desire and know that it won't be there much longer because it will have manifested. But as we know, life happens and something else will eventually be our focus, we'll have other lessons to learn or experience and life will continue on.

Letting go of the inner work and resistance you've held on to for so long can be a tricky one, so switch how you're looking at your big desires and prepare to receive. Accept that change is coming and that it's incredibly positive, because the very change you know needs to happen is welcoming in your desire, which you've worked so hard for. So enjoy this process and have fun, prepare in a way that feels good to you and remember that thoughts will come up and sometimes you will have to learn or heal some aspects on the job too. The learning doesn't just stop and I've very often had final layers to release after a desire has manifested in my life and that's been deeply healing in itself.

Expect the Unexpected

You will never be 100 per cent in the right place in your life to receive your desire, be fully healed or perfect – the manifestation of your desire *will* pleasantly surprise you and that's the magic and beauty of the Universe. The Universe always knows the perfect timing even if you can't see that just yet and it feels scary that it's right on the cusp, but use this as an invitation to transform this feeling into nervous excitement. How bloomin' exciting that your biggest dreams are right around the corner and very soon you'll look back and remember the days you prayed for these big blessings in your life! Think about anything that you may not have time or be able to do once your desire is here – and do those things! See your thoughts as being just thoughts and do the exercises that follow to help you relax into this preparing energy that's surrounding you.

This chapter has been setting you up for the embodiment of your desires and abundance, but I really want you to think about how you can embody this now that we're in the Healing stage. The embodiment of your desires will bring the same healing to your inner child as well, so how can your actions to prepare for your desires actively embody healing for your inner child too? Involve your inner child in this preparation process and embody the energy of your desires with your inner child.

Connect to the Core Energy of Your Desire

For your manifestation intention today, I wanted to add in a fun practice that my friend introduced me to a few years ago. This has been such a powerful tool for me and helped me manifest one of my biggest manifestations without even realizing it. It also ties into Chapter 15, "Aligned Manifesting and Abundance", perfectly and is a great way to hold the vision for your desire in an aligned way.

Connecting to the core energy of my desire felt weird at first, but little did I know how powerful this exercise really was! When manifesting my current relationship, my friend told me to stop putting faces, expectations, names or preferences to this guy and actually connect to the core energy of my desire. When I did, I was met with a beautiful red, warm energy that felt loving, kind and gentle. After seeing this energy for the first time I knew it was my desire and how good it felt – it felt aligned, it felt loving and it felt safe. It instantly relaxed my nervous system and that's how I knew it was in alignment. That energy didn't reflect the person I was dating at the time and sure enough that relationship fell away quickly after doing this practice.

Every now and again when I felt like it, I would spend time with the core energy – I'd talk to it, watch it and feel it come toward me naturally. When I met my now boyfriend, I remember a few months in thinking back to this core energy and being shocked, because it was the same as his energy – that kind, gentle, loving energy matched his energy completely and that's how I knew I'd manifested this relationship.

Connecting to the core energy of your desire can be used for any manifestation. The reason why I believe this is such an important manifestation tool is because it gets us out of our human mind and removes limitations, expectations and resistance. We essentially get out of our own way, get to the root outside of 3D constructs and open up to what the Universe is trying to bring into our life for the highest good. We think we may know what something looks like but when you're connecting to the core energy your intentions are pure and aligned to really what is for your highest good. This easy exercise opens up the gates for your desire to flow to you so much quicker as you drop your expectations and align with what's ready and waiting for you.

So below you'll find the steps for my "Connecting to the Core Energy of Your Desire" meditation – like I did, do this as often or as little as you'd like.

"Connecting to the Core Energy of Your Desire" Meditation

First of all, please make sure that you're sitting comfortably and close your eyes. Start to take a deep breath in and relax.

1. In your mind's eye, with your eyes closed, I want you to visualize your biggest manifestation in front of you now.

2. Next, still in your mind's eye or with your physical hand, I want you to start wiping away any human aspects to your desire (names, faces, locations, companies, etc.). Keep wiping all the human aspects away until you reach the core energy of your desire. For every person, the energy's colour will be different but its this colour that will let you know you have reached the core.

3. Once you have the core energy of your desire, take note of how it feels and how it's appearing to you and ask yourself: What colour is the core energy of my desire? What is the feeling/emotion or word that represents this energy? Are there any sounds or smells connected to the core energy? How does it make me feel being around the core energy of my desire?

4. Spend time with the core energy and ask it any questions if that feels good to you. Over time naturally (do not force this) invite this energy to come closer to you as you open your arms and welcome it in.

5. Once you've come out of this meditation, note down your answers to the above questions and make sure to do this practice as often as it feels right to.

⁺⁺ **PRACTICE** ⁺⁺

Journaling prompt
"How safe does it feel to receive this desire on a scale of 1 to 10?" (With 1 being not safe and 10 being completely safe.)

Intention
Complete the "Connecting to the Core Energy of Your Desire" meditation in this chapter as often as it feels good to.

Activity
Make a list in your notebook or journal of what you can do to prepare for your manifestation. Do you need to get yourself physically and energetically ready to receive? Is there anything you may need to purchase or prepare so you're ready to receive? Do you need to declutter your home to make space for this desire? Is this about finding balance in your life so you have the room already in your schedule? Write your list and start preparing to receive by taking action on these points while allowing yourself to open up and receive from the Universe. Allow yourself to be met halfway. Remember only to buy things when it feels aligned and good to do so. (This is part of my mindful spending teachings and a great tip to follow for manifesting money too!)

Action
Ask yourself the following:

- How can I shift my mindset into receiving now?
- What change am I resisting?
- How can I lean into this change and get excited by it?

Unconditional Love

At the foundation of everything we are and do in this lifetime is unconditional love. It's what we're born into this world with and the goal of our inner work and healing journey is to return home to ourselves and experience unconditional love.

I mentioned at the start of this book that I am a Life Path 33 in numerology. While I've known this for quite a few years now, it was never really explained to me properly until I met my numerologist friend and fellow author Kaitlyn, who told me what being a Life Path 33 really meant. Kaitlyn's explanation transformed my life, because finally my life, experiences and hurt made sense. The rarest number in numerology, the Life Path 33 is a Master Number, meaning these people have chosen a harder path in life to learn more alongside the other two Master Numbers, 11 and 22. Each Life Path Number has their own meaning and journey but the Life Path 33 is here to learn unconditional love and embody this fully. Also known as the enlightened nurturers and ultimate care-givers, Life Path 33s are here to be tested in love over and over again until they learn unconditional love for themselves first so that they are then able to give it to others. It's the number that represents love in its purest form.

Love has been my biggest test in this lifetime and this is originally what this book was going to be about. From day one, even before I wrote my first book, *Spiritual Queen*, I knew I wanted to write a book on love. Only being aged 23 at the time, I thought this was silly and knew one day the book would be birthed. I knew the book I had been envisioning was book number three. Over the 18 months it's taken me to write this book, the themes and focuses have all changed and have been choices I made before my publisher even saw my manuscript. I toyed with many ideas and deleted 20,000 words when I felt called to write the version you're reading now. I had many realizations along this journey about unconditional love and how our own inner journey is the only love book we ever need because, remember, the inner world always reflects the outer. The goal of this book and healing in general is to return to unconditional love and that's why this subject deserves its own chapter.

Despite my challenges in giving and receiving unconditional love throughout the years, I knew I didn't feel it for myself despite how much inner work I was doing. Kaitlyn's definition of my Life Path Number suddenly made my life and past experiences make sense and it felt like it had all been worth it.

At the very start of this book, I explained how we're born into this world with unconditional love and we don't know any difference when we're babies, yet our conditioning and environment slowly deflate that bubble of pure unconditional love as we grow into children and then, by our teenage years, we are programmed with beliefs, identities and stories that very often stop us from feeling or giving unconditional love. So how does this affect our manifestations? Well, when we radiate unconditional love we are aligned with the Universe and oneness, meaning we are putting out positive energy and have a joyful, happy frequency that we're emitting regularly. When we're not giving and receiving unconditional love in equal measure, we feel lack, control, fear, resistance and closed off, which equally gets reflected back to us.

I notice that when I feel aligned with unconditional love, abundance flows to me in all areas of life as I flow with life; but when I've not felt like a being of unconditional love or when I was in the Hurt or Healing phase of my journey, I experienced resistance, challenges and felt a lack of love in my life. So by opening up again and doing the inner work to help us return back to a state of experiencing unconditional love in life for ourselves and others, we can all open the flood gates for more magic, joy and abundance to flow to us with ease as we're vibrating at the frequency of unconditional love itself.

Love with Acceptance and Freedom

Unconditional love to me means unconditional peace and no judgement toward myself or others. It means having healthy boundaries and loving myself unconditionally. It means putting myself first and knowing my worth. It means becoming a being of love and helping others without the expectation of receiving. It means loving someone with all their flaws – and loving all my flaws too. This is just my definition and there are many ways to define what unconditional love means to you.

However we define it, the Universe itself is unconditional love and it's our job to remember this love and experience unconditional love in this lifetime. Now, that may seem impossible to some people reading this book, especially while being in the Hurt stage, as when we are hurt we forget what unconditional love is and feels like, but it is available for everyone and there is an unlimited supply when we unconditionally love ourselves.

Although I'd worked on self-care and self-love for years prior to my journey to unconditional love, self-worth for me was really the key to unlocking unconditional love and coming home to myself. I had to love every aspect of myself – my higher self, my shadow self, my inner child, my body and my past. Acceptance played a big part in this, and igniting that love for myself after so many years allowed me to embody self-worth and heal my wounds around love and self-worth.

When Luna, my dachshund, came into my life in 2021 I became a mum for the first time – even if it was a dog mum! Raising this little ball of unconditional love and joy showed me what it really meant to love another unconditionally and she has been healing for me in so many ways. I truly believe dogs, or any pets for that matter, are sent into our life to love us unconditionally. Dogs, for example, always forgive, love us unconditionally and want to be our best friend no matter what – they really are angels sent from the Universe. Seeing Luna's unconditional love then taught me how I needed to do this for myself and how there needs to be unconditional love at the core of any relationship with ourselves or others.

Unconditional love doesn't mean you don't have boundaries or you let people get away with things. Quite the opposite – but it's learning to embrace and accept our flaws, our imperfections, our mistakes, all the things we deem unacceptable and say, "I still love you anyway."

The key I've learned to unconditional love and even romantic relationships is freedom. Too often we try to control everything and we place judgement and fear onto our relationships. We can also project a variety of other emotions, such as anger and sadness, for example. This is what causes division and separation. When we can allow ourselves and others to be free and be our authentic self, this is unconditional love. When we place exceptions or conditions on our loved ones and ourselves, all we're doing is loving conditionally.

When I met my current partner after Luna came into my life, I knew I was in the right place to receive a healthy loving relationship, as unconditional love was all around me at this point and nothing fazed me anymore. My partner allows me to be free and my true self, and I allow him to do the same. And it's the easiest thing in the world when you have two people committed to growing together and who unconditionally love. That's not to say there aren't ups and downs because just like all aspects of life we experience seasons and the ebb and flow of life. But one thing that remains the same for me especially is accepting him, all of him – because it all makes him him! Which is a reminder of how we need to fully accept and love ourselves too.

I often see people jumping very quickly into new relationships after heartbreak, and while we can't always help when we meet people, I'm so grateful I took a year after my last relationship to date, to heal and to love myself so that I could be emotionally available and give my all to my current relationship. I made sure that I was someone I wanted to spend the rest of my life with first before I started looking for another relationship. The truth was, I was so hurt after my last relationship that I needed to do some deep inner work and rebuild myself once again before I got involved with anyone else. So I committed to the unknown, as I've described in earlier chapters, and committed to being happy and healthy in myself first so I knew that even if I didn't meet anyone I would be happy with myself and be my own soulmate.

Healing the Layers That Stop Us from Loving Unconditionally

When some people jump into new relationships, they once again seek someone to fix the void within themselves when really the problem will keep resurfacing in every relationship they have with their karmic partners until they address it themselves. This is why self-worth kept coming up for me time and time again until I learned to experience self-worth and unconditional love for myself.

Today, my relationship feels as easy as breathing and for the first time in my life I feel unconditionally happy, supported and loved – because I give that to myself too. You see, all along I kept finding men who said I was asking for too much and when I gave myself everything, an amazing guy came along who said, "That's all you need?" So if this is you right now after a break-up, take your time, there is no rush. Nurture yourself and become your own soulmate first and then the right people will come into your life when you least expect it.

The inner child also has a lot to do with our capacity for unconditional love, because what really shuts us off from giving and receiving unconditional love is our inner child and their beliefs and fears around this. So start off by accepting yourself fully and working on loving yourself wholeheartedly, which we covered in Part One, Hurt. When your inner child is heard, nurtured and happy, you will feel magic, unconditional love and joy in your day-to-day life as you both experience this love for one another.

Another key to unconditional love is to stay present and fall in love with here and now. We can't truly experience unconditional love unless we feel it here and now in this exact moment. So ask yourself today as you move into the Healed phase of this book and journey, "Do I feel in love in with my life here and now?" If the answer is "no" then there is your clue as to where some work may still need to be done.

I also want you to start becoming your own soulmate. We so often put the pressure of this title on one person when in fact we have dozens of soulmates whom we incarnate with in each lifetime and who are all our soul family. Some will be romantic lovers, others could be family members or even a pet – but you are your own soulmate too and this has to start with you. As the saying goes: "Be ~~with~~ someone who make you happy."

In terms of romantic love, as I mentioned earlier when talking about our divine assignments, the Universe will continue to send you karmic partners until you heal all the things preventing you from unconditionally loving yourself without the presence of a romantic partner. That's when a romantic soulmate can and *will* come in. Your divine assignments are your biggest mirrors in life – each time they are holding up a big mirror to you, giving you the opportunity to grow and learn. To evolve more into unconditional love and to soften the edges of our heart that have been hurt in the past.

Acknowledging Anger and Confusion

Even though we may be beings of unconditional love, this also doesn't mean that we won't experience shadow energy of anger and negativity. Even now I still experience anger sometimes, but it's different. Instead of the triggered, reactive anger that I used to feel, I now experience spiritual anger (a nonreactive anger) – which is an important emotion to express and is key to embodying the sacred divine feminine energy fully.

Anger isn't always negative; it's an emotion just like any other. We have a whole heap of emotions and all of them are perfectly okay to feel and express in an aligned way. Recently, I judged myself for feeling spiritual anger boiling over and spilling out, but it was a reminder for me that I will feel this from time to time and it's important to voice this and not shut it down until it overspills like a pressure cooker. When I was able to express this anger in a healthy way it instantly lost all its power over me. I witnessed that I didn't feel triggered and I didn't feel reactive like I used to, I actually just felt pissed and that's okay.

Anger and confusion very often lead to breakthroughs and growth so giving and receiving unconditional love doesn't mean we don't experience anger, sadness or a bad day; it just means we're able to witness these things with more acceptance and work with them in a healthier way, where we can say, "I feel really mad right now but I still love myself anyway", or, "I feel sad and unhappy right now but I still love myself anyway." Even if in that moment it doesn't create a big shift just by saying this, small shifts will happen as you chose the path of non-judgement and acceptance. But it's easier said than done when you have triggering and reactiveness underneath the surface, and this is why it's so important to identify what sacred anger is over reactive anger and use the tools in this book to release any triggers or wounds underneath the anger.

The Never-ending Journey of Unconditional Love

The journey to unconditional love is lifelong. I don't for a moment think I have it all figured out as it's my lifelong lesson and journey. However, I do have the understanding, awareness and tools now to navigate this in a healthier and more conscious manner, no matter what comes my way, and I hope you too have found these tools and modalities within this book.

Returning to unconditional love is something we have to check in with often and self-reflect on what may be stopping us from giving or receiving it. So although you may feel and be experiencing unconditional love now, that doesn't mean you won't have a season when you may have to work on it that little bit harder. As long as you're being your own soulmate, chances are that unconditional love is going to be flowing in your life – and your divine assignments will also reflect this to you too.

Through our romantic and platonic relationships, every divine connection will challenge us to love unconditionally at every stage of our life, and to drop our judgements and our expectations and embrace others for who they are truly meant to be. Unconditional love places no restraints or conditions on us so if you feel you do this in your relationships, there is absolutely a limiting belief or fear underneath this.

We may not be able to understand or agree with everything our loved ones bring to the table of life but we can still love them anyway. Just like our pets love us no matter what, we can do that too. After all, as humans, unconditional love is what we were born to be and experience – it's our true essence as spiritual beings. Because when we strip away this human experience and look at the Universe, Source and our souls, all we're left with is unconditional love.

When our loved ones pass over, they only feel unconditional love as they have returned to Source and are their true being (their higher self) again. The blocks, resistance and conditioning they experienced as a human completely disappears as they leave this identity and return back to oneness. Oneness means seeing yourself in others and knowing we are all connected and the same. It can be hard to get your head around this when there are so many injustices in the world and people operating from low energy, but even they were born into this world as beings of unconditional love and will return to Source as one too.

We have been conditioned to believe that giving unconditional love can make us weak or susceptible to people using and abusing us, and while, yes, people could take your good nature for granted, that has everything to do with them and not you. As a being of unconditional love, this means you have strong and healthy boundaries too.

We need to redefine how we see unconditional love and embrace our vulnerability more, along with the softening of our hearts and minds as we open up to this energy again. Softening or even being vulnerable can feel like a lot to ask of you, especially after you've experienced trauma or hurt, but what this entire book and journey are really about is returning you home, to unconditional love, and opening your heart again in whatever way that resonates with you through the three stages of Hurt, Healing and Healed. Everyone around you will thrive and reflect this back to you when you amplify this energy.

Finally, to wrap up this chapter with a yummy practice for the heart, I've included an Unconditional Love Wheel, below, for you to colour in and explore. After completing your wheel, look at which areas you may need to spark more unconditional love in and take action toward improving these. Now that you've done all of the incredible healing work in this book, it's time to spark joy, love and magic in the whole of your life!

✦ PRACTICE ✦

Journaling prompts
- "Do I want to spend the rest of my life with myself?"
- "Do I feel in love in with my life here and now?"

Intention
As our last manifesting intention in this section I want you to either repeat the affirmation below or create your own. Repeat this over the next 21 days to yourself in the mirror or write it down and repeat it once a day, and see what manifests in your life as a result of your hard work:

I commit to keeping my heart open to giving and receiving unconditional love. Pure love surrounds me each and every day and I call in loving experiences, abundance and joy wherever I go. It is safe for me to be and experience unconditional love.

Activity
Complete the Unconditional Love Wheel on the next page or draw your own in your notebook. Now colour it in from 1 to 10 (with 1 being "not very" and 10 being "full of unconditional love") to rate how much unconditional love you are receiving and experiencing currently in each area of your life. After completing your wheel look at which areas you may need to spark more unconditional love in and take action toward improving these. Using this wheel to guide yourself, you could journal on how you can spark more love in these areas with yourself and others, moving forward.

Action
Become your own soulmate in whatever way feels right to you. You may want to revisit Chapter 10, "Self-care, Self-love and Self-worth", to work on any resistance. Look at what stops you from being your own soulmate currently and continue to work on your relationship with yourself and your inner child. Spark as much unconditional love in your life as possible from now on to help create more fun and joy and bring your desires into fruition.

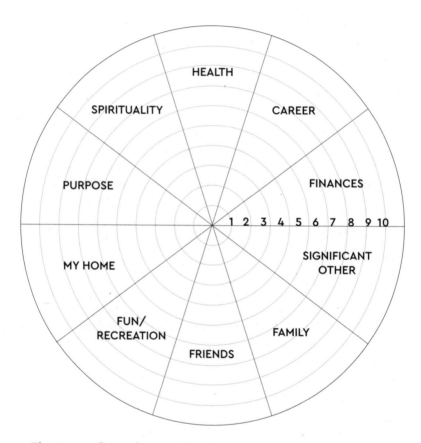

The Unconditional Love Wheel

Healed Check-in

Once you've completed Part Three, journal on the questions below either here or in a notebook of your choice.

What are you biggest takeaways from this section?

_____

_____

_____

What three things will you implement from this section?

_____

_____

_____

What have you discovered within yourself through the Healed section?

_____

_____

_____

What daily practices are you going to add into your morning routine consistently?

_____

_____

_____

What happy things have you noticed about yourself throughout this journey?

_____

_____

_____

What aligned abundance/manifestations have come into your life during this process?

_____

_____

_____

How can you continue to prepare for your manifestation?

_____

_____

_____

How can you maintain balance in your life moving forward?

_____

_____

_____

What key takeaway are you going to take forward from this _Hurt, Healing, Healed_ journey?

_____

_____

_____

Rating Scale

Circle your score from 1 to 10 (with 1 being "not very happy" and 10 being "very happy").

Happiness:	1	2	3	4	5	6	7	8	9	10
Self-love:	1	2	3	4	5	6	7	8	9	10
Fulfilment:	1	2	3	4	5	6	7	8	9	10
Self-worth:	1	2	3	4	5	6	7	8	9	10
Confidence:	1	2	3	4	5	6	7	8	9	10
Gratefulness:	1	2	3	4	5	6	7	8	9	10

Healed Total   =   /60

Moving Forward

As I approach the end of this 18-month journey of deep healing and transformation in writing this book, my nan transitioned back to source today.

I had been feeling like this conclusion was stuck and there was a missing puzzle piece. Nan has been a pivotal part of my healing journey and my mother line – so to be sitting here today feeling love and peace toward her, as she transitions back to love and Source, feels deeply healing itself.

During our years alive together, Nan and I may not have always had the connection I wish we'd had, but in the last few months I've been on a deep journey down my ancestral and mother line with Family Constellations (see Resources, page 209). I was able to find healing and understand why certain events and trauma happened in my family. I'm grateful she is now at peace with her husband and that she doesn't have to live in pain anymore – although we never talked about it Earthside, I hope this book has been a conversation between us.

Thank you, Nan, for bringing my mum into the world and for allowing me to learn the lessons I needed to with you. I will always remember our happy times together in my childhood and this book is in loving memory of you.

And so it is.

As you and I reach the end of our journey together here, I want to remind you that this really is the beginning and not an ending. The healing journey is a lifelong one, but as we ebb and flow through the seasons of change and growth we'll experience periods of lighter joy and abundance, and periods of inner growth, expansion and reflection. Over your lifetime you will have multiple "awakenings" and discover a new version of yourself each and every year. You will grow, expand, contract and release all in your own beautiful time and phases, and there is no rush or comparison here because only you will ever experience your journey here on Earth.

Throughout this book I've guided you through the three pillars (practical, cognitive and spiritual – mind, body, spirit) and stages of healing (Hurt, Healing and Healed). I really hope this book has helped you to discover what has been stopping you from manifesting your desires and has helped you to unlock and identify powerful healing work that you've taken action with and released. I hope that by now you feel lighter, brighter and at peace from completing all the chapters and practices in this book. I also hope that you are blossoming into a new version of yourself as you reach the Healed stage and are seeing manifestations flow to you and the fulfilment of your wildest dreams. I hope that you feel abundant and I hope that you feel hope and excitement for all that's to come.

Eighteen months ago, I started writing this book at the beginning of the pandemic and how this book has transformed in that period has been incredible to witness. How much I've grown, healed and changed in this time has also felt so special. When I accepted the assignment of this book from the Universe I definitely couldn't have predicted the journey I would go down and the outcome and abundance I would have, sitting here now. I feel so grateful and blessed to have lived the journey with you and worked with some incredible souls along the way to heal myself and return back to peace, harmony and unconditional love.

If I'd have known this would be how I'd end up finishing this book all that time ago, I wouldn't have believed you. I was in a total opposite place in my life where I felt stuck, hopeless and didn't know what was going to happen for me. Now I'm sitting here free from the past, free from the wounds, limiting beliefs and fears that once held me back. I've manifested incredible abundance into my life and I now have my little Luna and an amazing boyfriend, both of whom I never imagined I would be lucky enough to have 18 months ago.

My intention for my 28th birthday was to be free from the past and to find peace – and once again the Universe delivered. Who knew it would come from nearly two years of intense inner work? At points I felt like I would never see light again but slowly and surely I did feel like me again – a brand new me. The Universe supported me in ways it hadn't before and I finally came back home to myself. And I hope that this is your takeaway from the book too.

I often joke to the authors that I work with that when they write their book they will live it during the writing process – and once again this book has been just that for me. It's been my deepest, most expansive work to date but I'm so proud of myself for committing and showing up for myself and for you, reading this book. This is what I want to express to you too: that I am so proud of you for getting this far and finishing the book, because in 18 months' time you too will also look back and think, "Wow, I really have come a long way!" All it took was that intention for me and a desire to write this book for you all; then the rest became a beautiful journey that unfolded and set me free.

Alignment is a practice, not a destination – the experience of writing this book has felt backward to me compared to my other books, as I've had to unravel and unlearn the process with you. Although we can reach new heights of awareness, healing and alignment, don't judge your success based on a destination, but base it on how you feel right here and now. The destination or manifestation will come in its own perfect timing, but remember that alignment takes consistency and practice from you. It takes regular honesty, pivotal moments and moments of reflection. Now you have the tools to navigate this, remember your life is an ongoing, beautiful piece of art. Expect miracles and expect your capacity and alignment to receive miracles to increase.

The key to seeing consistent results is to be consistent, so please don't put this book down and forget the magic that we've created here. You've come so far and achieved so much through this that it's important to walk your talk now and live this version of yourself. Keep up your daily practice and use this book as a manual for life when something does come up. Make a list of your favourite practices that you'd like to continue and any that you really saw big shifts with, so that you can revisit them when you need them. See this book as being a life companion to support and hold you whenever you need it, and you could also pass it on to someone you know or even a stranger to share this positivity with.

Let's have a recap now of the three pillars of healing so that you can see how you've moved through each layer and made massive shifts during this book. Use these pillars to check in and see where you are emotionally as a friendly reminder and guide, moving forward. As Gabby Bernstein shares, it's not about how often you get hurt but how quickly you can get back home. Gently remind yourself of this, Queen, when any challenges arise in the future.

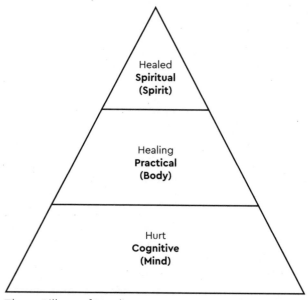

Three Pillars of Healing

What has really helped me during my healing journey has been focusing energy back onto myself, which was never about manifesting a partner, a dog or any of the incredible career success I've achieved over the years. It was about feeling peace and at home within myself, being my own best friend and releasing the blocks and resistance that held me back for many years. I was able to see why I'd attracted certain relationships into my life and what the karmic lesson was; I was able to witness my own behaviours and stop these in their tracks. The truth is, we all want to feel and experience love in all areas of our life and within ourselves – and the way to return to manifest that is by releasing the blocks and the conditioning that has taught us how to block unconditional love.

Love connects us all; it's what runs deep within the veins of everyone. Just as sadness and fear connect us also, we can choose to be love, let love in and return to love. Love is our essence and our being, it's what we were born to do; so while this book isn't about finding romantic love, it's about way more than that. It's about reconnecting you back to love, true unconditional love, so that you can remember that love is all around you and it always has been.

The love that you have created within yourself will reflect in your outer world and all your experiences. Love is at the core of manifestation and when we feel love within ourselves and for the outer world the whole game shifts. You win. You succeed and you magnetize. True alignment is in the frequency of unconditional love, so the more inner work you do to remove resistance, the lighter, brighter and more expansive you will feel. Abundance then pours into your life and you manifest from a different place, a different octave.

Thank you for putting your trust in me with this book, thank you for reading it and allowing me to facilitate this healing for you. Take a moment to breathe in the gratitude for yourself also, for completing this book and for committing to yourself and growth – what an incredible achievement! I'm forever grateful for the opportunity to write books as it makes my soul so happy, so thank you for always being my biggest supporters and one epic online family. The love and support you show me and others in this community always fills my heart with so much joy.

Because, you see, this *is* a book about love just as I envisioned it to be all those years ago. Really, all we have to remember is that everything always comes back to love. Love is all around us if only we remember to turn the light back on in our hearts and let it in. Love truly does conquer all and, as we've explored in this book, all we need to go through the three stages of healing and achieve our heart's desires and dreams is love – *true unconditional love.*

Acknowledgements

What a journey this book has been! For so long, I couldn't see this coming together, so to now see it in its final glory feels surreal but magical! I want to take this opportunity to thank everyone who has made this book possible.

I want to thank my nearest and dearest friends (you know who you are) and my parents for all your continued support, love and healing you enrich my life with. I am so blessed to have you all in my life and I love you all so much. Thank you to The Happy Mermaids for also helping me along this book journey and for holding the space for me. Thank you to Luna and my wonderful boyfriend for coming into my life during this book journey and for healing and loving me in ways I never thought possible. Thank you for also being my muses in this book and for supporting me and my work.

And of course the wonderful team at Watkins – thank you, Anya, for once again believing in my work, and Laura, Fiona, Brittany, Monica, Vicky and Rachel for making this work a dream and for being the best publishing team, full of positivity, support and love. I feel honoured and proud to have the best team around me who are all so inspiring. Thank you to Donna also for being my right-hand woman for two years, my PR manager and friend. You saw me go through this journey and kept cheerleading me throughout – thank you for helping me navigate the business, this book and life.

Last but certainly not least I want to thank you my incredible community and followers! Without you none of this would be possible and this book is for you. Thank you for supporting me, trusting in my work and for being so blooming nice. Every time I interact with you, whether it's in my online containers or even in person, I am blown away by just how kind, positive and lovely you all are. It's an honour having you here and facilitating this work for you. I feel so lucky to have you here and to witness all of your beautiful transformations daily. Thank you also to my awesome clients who allowed me to share their stories in this book. Every day I wake up and feel incredibly lucky to do what I do for a living and you all make it so special and magical every day – thank you, thank you, thank you.

Resources

In some ways, we've only scratched the surface of healing in this book, as, of course, there is only so much I can include in these pages. While writing *Hurt, Healing, Healed* I went on a deep and expansive journey to heal my own wounds and also to explore numerous modalities for research and healing purposes – a journey of discovery that still continues. So that's why I want to share with you some healing modalities I worked with throughout writing this book, which allowed me to go on my own *Hurt, Healing, Healed* journey. These are some great stepping stones to look into once you've finished the book and explore if you feel called to ...

IEMT (Integral Eye Movement Therapy)

What I used it for: PTSD, inner child work, releasing trauma and fears

What it is: IEMT is a talk-free healing modality where the therapist helps you to desensitize traumatic memories and fears from the past using your eyes. Similar to EMDR (Eye Movement Desensitization and Reprocessing), this is a great way to heal traumatic memories without having to talk about them. I found this one of the quickest and most powerful modalities and would highly recommend it to anyone!

Family Constellations

What I used it for: ancestral and mother line healing
What it is: I first came across this concept on Gwyneth Paltrow's "Goop Lab" and instantly knew I had to try it. Family Constellations is a therapeutic approach designed to help reveal the hidden dynamics in a family or relationship in order to address any stressors impacting these relationships and heal them. This alternative approach may help people seeking treatment view their concerns from a different perspective, and therapists may offer the Family Constellations approach as a treatment for issues proving difficult to treat with traditional therapy. This alternative approach was developed by German psychotherapist Bert Hellinger in the mid-1990s. Family Constellations therapy evolved out of his work as a family therapist and his belief in the energy, both positive and negative, found in familial bonds. I love this modality because we carry around so much stuff that isn't ours and doing this showed me how some fears and beliefs weren't always actually my own. From doing these sessions I found healing with my mother line, closure and released big fears I'd carried around my entire life.

The Emotion and Body Code

What I used it for: releasing limiting beliefs and fears, energy work, health and clearing blocks
What it is: The Emotion Code® was created by Dr Bradley Nelson. Understanding that our bodies store trapped emotions really was the missing puzzle piece for me in my healing journey. I've worked on so many different aspects of my life over the last year – from abundance blocks to releasing trauma, limiting beliefs and fears and trapped emotions in my body, which were manifesting as hormonal acne in my physical body.

Past-life Regression

What I used it for: releasing karmic contracts and limiting beliefs and fears I knew weren't mine after doing the inner work in this lifetime.
What it is: during a past-life regression session with a trained specialist using hypnotherapy, you relax and are then guided into the past life that is relevant to your current life issue. You are guided the entire way and are fully awake and aware at

all points. I've found these sessions really fun and exciting to explore and have even Googled key times and events that came up afterwards – to find they match my past-life memories! These sessions are so beneficial for anyone with an irrational fear or who can't pinpoint where their limiting belief or fear comes from in this lifetime.

I hope by sharing the extra modalities that I've used on my journey, they will inspire you to explore and that you will have even more incredible healing results if you'd like extra support from myself or the modalities I've mentioned above. Some other great modalities I'd recommend exploring are sound healing (gong baths and sound bowls), chakra work and Reiki. I also highly recommend EFT (Emotional Freedom Technique), especially Brad Yates's videos on this subject on YouTube.

Important links

Throughout this book I have mentioned various links for meditations, etc. Please find them listed below.

- To purchase the *Hurt Healing Healed* meditation playlist, please see my website: www.emmamumford.co.uk/shop

- To listen to my heart chakra meditation please see my website: www.emmamumford.co.uk/hurthealinghealed

- To download the permission slip I mention on page 61, please see my website: www.emmamumford.co.uk/hurthealinghealed

- To watch my daily energy protection meditations, or any of my other videos, please see my YouTube channel: /EmmaMumford

- To access my "Inner Child Joy" course, please see: www.emmamumford.co.uk/innerchildjoy/

Further Reading

Bradshaw, John, *Homecoming: Reclaiming and Championing Your Inner Child*, Piatkus, London, 1999

Brown, Brené, *Daring Greatly: How the Courage to Be Vulnerable Transforms the Way We Live, Love, Parent, and Lead*, Penguin, London, 2015

Hay, Louise, *You Can Heal Your Life*, Hay House, London, 1984

LePera, Nicole, *How To Do The Work: Recognise Your Patterns, Heal from Your Past, Create Your Self*, Orion, London, 2021

Nelson, Bradley, *The Emotion Code: How to Release Your Trapped Emotions for Abundant Health, Love and Happiness*, Vermilion, London, 2019

Van Der Kolk, Bessel, *The Body Keeps the Score: Mind, Brain and Body in the Transformation of Trauma*, Penguin, London, 2015

Williamson, Marianne, *A Return To Love: Reflections on the Principles of 'A Course in Miracles'*, Harper Thorsons, London, 2015

Winfrey, Oprah and Bruce Perry, *What Happened to You?: Conversations on Trauma, Resilience, and Healing*, Bluebird, 2021

Wolynn, Mark, *It Didn't Start With You: How Inherited Family Trauma Shapes Who We Are and How to End the Cycle*, Penguin, London, 2016

About the Author

Emma Mumford is the UK's leading Law of Attraction expert. She is an award-winning life coach and mentor, Law of Attraction YouTuber, the bestselling author of *Positively Wealthy* and *Spiritual Queen*, speaker and host of the popular podcast "Spiritual Queen's Badass Podcast". Emma's work helps people turn their dream life into an abundant reality using the Law of Attraction and spirituality. Through her work, Emma has helped hundreds of thousands of people globally over the last decade.

Emma started her money-saving journey to abundance back in 2013. After finding couponing in her hour of need – thanks to her ex-boyfriend leaving her with his £7,000 debt – Emma then set up the nationally popular brand Extreme Couponing and Deals UK Ltd and became known as the UK's Coupon Queen. In 2016, Emma underwent a spiritual awakening and knew that her calling in life was to move away from her money-saving roots and grow into the personal development world with her own brand. Emma has since sold her first business and now focuses on her spiritual business full-time.

www.emmamumford.co.uk | @iamemmamumford

WATKINS

Sharing Wisdom Since 1893

The story of Watkins began in 1893, when scholar of esotericism John Watkins founded our bookshop, inspired by the lament of his friend and teacher Madame Blavatsky that there was nowhere in London to buy books on mysticism, occultism or metaphysics. That moment marked the birth of Watkins, soon to become the publisher of many of the leading lights of spiritual literature, including Carl Jung, Rudolf Steiner, Alice Bailey and Chögyam Trungpa.

Today, the passion at Watkins Publishing for vigorous questioning is still resolute. Our stimulating and groundbreaking list ranges from ancient traditions and complementary medicine to the latest ideas about personal development, holistic wellbeing and consciousness exploration. We remain at the cutting edge, committed to publishing books that change lives.

DISCOVER MORE AT:

www.watkinspublishing.com

Read our blog

Watch and listen to
our authors in action

Sign up to
our mailing list

We celebrate conscious, passionate, wise and happy living.
Be part of that community by visiting

 /watkinspublishing    @watkinswisdom

 /watkinsbooks    @watkinswisdom